S0-AIJ-244

Dark Harvest

DARK HARVEST

*Migrant Farmworkers
in America*

Brent Ashabranner

Photographs by Paul Conklin

LINNET BOOKS
1993

Text copyright © 1985 by Brent Ashabranner.
Photographs copyright © 1985 by Paul Conklin.
All rights reserved.
Published 1993 by Linnet Books,
an imprint of The Shoe String Press, Inc.
North Haven, Connecticut 06473.

Library of Congress Cataloging-in-Publication Data

Ashabranner, Brent K., date
Dark harvest.
Includes index.
1. Migrant agricultural laborers—United States—Juvenile literature
I. Title.
HD1525.A87   1993   331.5'44'0973   93-33170
ISBN 0-208-02391-7 cl.

The paper in this publication meets the minimum
requirements of the American National Standard for
Information Sciences—Permanence of Paper for Printed
Library Materials.
ANSI Z39.48—1984. ⊗

Printed in the United States of America.

For Susan
who helped in many ways

Contents

Acknowledgments

MANY PEOPLE helped us in gathering the material for this book. In addition to those persons mentioned in the text, we would like to thank Hank Aguirre, Department of Health and Human Services, Washington, D. C.; Ken Butler, Superintendent of Federal Programs, Somerset County, Maryland; Kathy Fox, Cornell Migrant Program, Wayne County, New York; Charlie Horwitz and Steve Nagler, Migrant Legal Action Program, Washington, D. C.; Barbara Mainster, Redlands Christian Migrant Association, Immokalee, Florida; Rosemary Salazar, Hispanic Affairs, U.S. Catholic Conference, Washington, D. C.; Morris Sorbello, Oswego Growers and Shippers, Inc., New York; Rob Williams, Florida Rural Legal Services, Immokalee; Thelma Waters, Migrant Head Start Program, Indiantown, Florida.

Steve Greenberg, Director, New York State Migrant Child Care Program, opened the doors of the program's splendid migrant child-care centers to us. Connie Castiglia, Regional Coordinator, was our wise and effective contact with migrants and growers in Wayne and Oswego counties. Kay Alteri, Ella O'Brien and Cheryl Van Kourenberg are other members of the New York program who were most helpful.

Sister JoEllen Shannon, S. P., and Jane Holland of the East Coast Migrant Head Start Project, Arlington, Virginia, shared their insights and information with us on many occasions. Early talks with Deborah Hudson and Marie Smith, migrant farm-workers on the Project's parents' council, were especially helpful.

Finally, we would like to thank Melissa Ashabranner for first suggesting that this book should be written and David Conklin for printing the photographs for it.

1
The Invisible People

Juan Medina, who runs a day-care center in Nocatee, Florida.

THE CUCUMBER fields we visited that morning were a few miles from Nocatee, a little town near the Gulf Coast in south Florida. Juan Medina, director of a Head Start day-care center for the children of migrant farmworkers, had offered to take us to the fields and introduce us to Daniel Cortez, a crew leader. We had learned quickly in our work on this book that you don't get anywhere with migrants, the crew leaders they work for, or the growers who hire the crew leaders without an intro-duction from someone they trust.

The sun was dazzling and almost directly overhead when we reached the fields a few minutes before noon. Paul was worried that the light was too bright and the sun in the wrong position for taking good pictures. In the years of working with him, I have learned that light, or the absence of it, dominates the thinking, emotions, and even the life of a professional photographer. I can predict Paul's moods with pinpoint accuracy any morning by

3

Picking cucumbers in the hot Florida sun.

looking out the window and seeing what kind of light we are likely to have that day.

The workers were on their lunch break when we arrived, about thirty of them gathered around their cars at the edge of a field. Daniel Cortez, his wife, and their sons were eating tortillas, chunks of roasted meat, and jalapeño peppers, using the hood of their pickup truck as a table. They offered us ice-cold Pepsi-Colas from a cooler in the back of the truck, and I explained to the crew leader who Paul and I were and that we were writing and photographing a book about migrant farmworkers in America. If he and the workers had no objections, I said, Paul would like to take some pictures and I would like to watch the work in the fields. I handed Cortez a copy of one of our recent books, *The New Americans,* which is about immigrants today.

Cortez listened and turned the pages of the book. He spoke briefly with Juan Medina in Spanish and then told me it would be all right. He said that some of the workers had children in Juan's day-care center.

Cortez told us that the crew was working for the minimum wage of $3.35 an hour today rather than being paid for the number of buckets of cucumbers they picked, as they usually were. The reason was that this was the second picking of the field, and they could make very little money picking by the bucket. The grower who owned the fields had wanted to plow the vines under because he couldn't make any money from a second picking, but Cortez had persuaded him to let his crew have the extra day's work at hourly wages.

"They will work hard, but I have told them they don't have to kill themselves," he said with a little shrug.

I talked with Cortez's son Daniel, Jr., a nineteen-year-old who drives a truck for his father. He had quit school and gone to work as a picker three years ago when his father was injured in a field accident. Only his mother was working then, and with three children besides himself, the family had to have more money. It was a familiar story but with a happier ending than most. His father had recovered and was now a crew leader with two trucks of his own.

"Did you go back to school?" I asked Daniel, Jr.

"No," he said.

Several of the field hands gathered around while we talked with Cortez and his son. They looked at our book curiously, especially the pictures showing recent immigrants from Mexico working on Texas and California farms.

One of the young men who had heard me talking with Cortez said to me, "Why do you want to write a book about us?"

"Because the work migrant farmworkers do is important," I said.

That was just the beginning of an explanation I intended to make, but the young man looked puzzled and walked back to the cucumber field. Within a few minutes the entire crew had returned to work. Paul went with them and began taking pictures. Most of the laborers were young Hispanic men and women, but there were a few Anglos and a few older workers. At first some of them joked about getting their picture in a book, but they soon forgot Paul and concentrated on filling their plastic buckets with cucumbers.

Cortez was right. Even though they were being paid hourly wages, they worked with a steady intensity, moving down the deep furrows between the rows of low vines. They bent forward from the waist, picking the large, mature cucumbers, leaving the ones that were spoiled or underdeveloped. Both hands worked together like parts of a machine, but a human machine that could select as well as pick.

As quickly as a worker filled a bucket, he would hoist it to his shoulder, carry it to the truck that rolled slowly down an unplowed strip between the rows, and pass it up to one of two girls on the truck bed. She would dump the cucumbers into one of the big boxes on the truck and pass the bucket back. The worker would hurry back to his place in the row and begin the routine all over again.

Even in early December the sun was hot, but not more than half the workers wore hats. Insects in the fields were a constant nuisance, and some people had long-sleeved shirts buttoned around their wrists despite the heat. Many of the workers wore long yellow gloves as protection against the cucumbers, which prick the fingers, making them swell and bleed. Most of the young men, however, ignored sun, bugs, and cucumber stickers and worked stoically in only jeans and T-shirts.

Occasionally someone carrying a bucket of cucumbers to the truck would take a few seconds for a drink of water from a barrel on the truck bed. A single plastic cup was tied to the barrel.

"Not very sanitary," I said to Juan Medina.

"No," he agreed, and added, "when I used to pick bell peppers, we would cut the top off of one and drink out of it, but you can't drink out of a cucumber."

I noticed that no portable toilet was anywhere in sight. "What do people do when they have to relieve themselves?" I asked.

"The men use the fields," Juan said.

"What about the women?"

"They wait until they get home, sometimes nine or ten hours."

"And if they can't wait?"

Juan shrugged. The answer was obvious.

There was nothing unusual about these working conditions at Nocatee. They were the norm for the great majority of fields and orchards that Paul and I had visited in different parts of the country. I had learned that there are very few laws to protect farmworkers from unsanitary and unhealthful conditions in the fields and that states that have such laws do little to enforce them. The U.S. Department of Labor for years has refused to set health and sanitation standards for farmworkers, although all other occupational groups in America have them.

This cheerful young migrant in southern Florida balances a tub of cucumbers on her shoulder. Despite her smile, it is very hard work.

When we left the cucumber fields a couple of hours later, several of the workers waved good-bye to us. "They're happy today because they have work," Juan Medina said. "Tomorrow they may not have any."

I saw the young man who had asked me why I wanted to write a book about migrant farmworkers, but he was busy picking and did not look up. I thought about his question on the drive back to Nocatee just as I had thought about it many times before. Why did I want to write this book? Why did Paul want to take the pictures for it?

What I told the young worker was true enough. Migrants' work in harvesting the country's fruits and vegetables is important, an indispensable part of the vast agricultural industry in America. That perhaps was sufficient reason for a book, but it was the migrants themselves that had kept us working on this book.

We came to know most of them as decent people, hard-working people who want to make an honest living for themselves and their families. They are people caught in a system that is often unfair, often cruel, but a system they are powerless to change without help from others.

Migrant farmworkers have been called the invisible people. They labor on squash and bean farms within an hour's drive of the opulence and glitter of Miami's gold coast, but visitors to that city seldom see them. They pick tomatoes and apples a few miles from Washington, D.C., but few residents of the nation's capital know they are there.

Migrant labor camps usually are located deep inside large farms, where the workers are not likely to be seen by outsiders. If migrants live in towns close to where they work, they occupy rundown houses in parts of the community most people try to avoid. Strangers wherever they go, they are treated like strangers and keep the company of their own kind.

Migrants are invisible in other ways. Because they are always on the move, they have no political base and little representation

Decrepit migrant housing on the outskirts of Immokalee, Florida.

in Congress or state legislatures. Very few have Social Security, unemployment insurance, or health insurance. They fall through these protective nets that society provides for most of its members. They are invisible to government. Many migrant farmworkers have entered the United States illegally from Mexico or other countries and want to be invisible to border patrols and immigration officials.

The isolation of migrants in American society has led to many stereotypes about them based on ignorance: They are shiftless, unreliable, unintelligent, have no ambition, work only when they need money for cheap wine or whiskey. These untruths, or half-truths that apply to only a few, keep migrant farmworkers from being seen as they really are. That is the most damaging invisibility.

We hope this book will make them more visible. That is the reason for it.

2
Following the Crops

Joel and Diana Villarreal with their daughter, Marlen, in La Grulla, Texas.

L A GRULLA is a village in Texas, almost on the banks of the Rio Grande, which forms the border with Mexico. La Grulla was named for a bird, a sandhill crane that migrates, and it is a good name for the little town. Most of the people who live there are Mexican-Americans whose parents migrated from their original homes south of the border, and most residents of La Grulla today are migrant farmworkers who spend much of the year harvesting crops in other parts of the country. In times past even the mayor of La Grulla joined the migrant streams.

In this small border town, different only in name from scores of others along the great river, live Joel and Diana Villarreal and their five-year-old daughter, Marlen. Their house, which Joel built with the help of his father, is small and tidy, the walls decorated with religious pictures and family photographs. It is a home they would like to live in all year long. For the past three years, however, they have closed it in April, packed their station wagon with clothes, blankets, dishes, and food, and made the long drive to the asparagus and strawberry fields of Washington State. They have returned to the life they knew as children when they traveled with their migrant farmworker parents.

Paul met the Villarreals when he was on a photographic assignment in Texas. "We did not want to go back to the fields," Joel told him, "but what else could we do? There is no other way for us to survive."

Their hopes had been high. They both graduated from high school, which not many migrant children do, and they believed that they could make a life that would not mean moving themselves and their children from one fruit or vegetable harvest to the next. After they were married, Joel found a job in a store in the nearby town of McAllen, but he lost it soon in the hard times that followed devaluation of the Mexican peso. For many American merchants on the border, the peso is almost as important as the dollar.

Joel managed to find enough work around La Grulla to hold on there for three years, but then he and Diana knew that they must go on the road again. There just was not enough money for food, clothes, and even the small light and heat bills for their little house.

This year they will begin their work cutting asparagus for Green Giant in Pasco, Washington. The trip north to Pasco takes three days, driving day and night without rest. Money is too precious to spend on a motel, and only Marlen in the backseat will get any real sleep. They will travel in a caravan with three or four other La Grulla families also going to work for Green Giant. All were recruited by the same labor contractor. Their cars are big because they must carry so much: clothes for both cold and hot weather, dishes and pans, and even as much food as possible because it is cheaper in La Grulla than on the road. Although the cars are big, they are not new. If one breaks down, other members of the caravan will help.

Joel Villarreal, along with a neighbor, plots out a course which he will follow on the long drive from La Grulla, Texas, to Washington State, where Joel and his wife will pick asparagus.

"You know when it gets bad?" Joel asked. "It's the night of the second day. You're someplace in Utah. You're tired and your back hurts and you want to pull off the road and just fall asleep behind the wheel, but you can't. You keep on driving."

At Pasco, Joel and Diana will work for two months, seven days a week if the crop and weather are good. Asparagus grows quickly and spoils if it is not harvested daily. They will work ten hours or more every day, ten hours of walking up and down sandy slopes filling the yellow boxes that hold about twenty pounds of asparagus. The constant stooping is terrible on the back and legs.

Asparagus is a delicate and temperamental plant. It must be cut exactly right with a sharp knife called a pica. A careless worker can cut himself badly. And if you get stuck with a bad plot, where some of the asparagus doesn't measure up to the company's grading standards, it is hard to make much money. But if things work out the way they are supposed to, an asparagus cutter can earn thirty-five dollars a day. For Joel and Diana together, that could be close to four thousand dollars for the asparagus season, and they will save as much as possible for the months with little or no income in La Grulla.

After the asparagus has been cut, they will move on to Mt. Vernon, Washington, for the short, intense strawberry season. It is almost a relief to pick strawberries, since different muscles are used, but the rows of plants seem to stretch on forever. "It is better not to look down the row," Diana said to Paul. "It is better to keep your eyes on the ground."

Except for the differences in cutting asparagus and picking strawberries, life is about the same for Joel and Diana in Mt. Vernon as it is in Pasco. The days begin before dawn and end at dark. The work camps where they live are silent by eight o'clock every night.

"Work and sleep," Diana said. "That is all we do."

When they leave Washington, Joel and Diana will drive to Oklahoma to hoe cotton. In the burning Oklahoma summer and early fall, cotton may be the hardest work of all, and the pay is not as good as it is for cutting asparagus and picking strawberries. But they will be glad to be there because they will be nearer to their home. When their work is finished in October, they will drive back to La Grulla, and Joel will try to find some work; but the money they have saved will help them through the winter months.

Joel and Diana know that next year they will have to follow

the crops again, and probably the next year and the next. But they have not lost hope that the time will come when, in April, they do not have to pack their car and start on the long road north.

Why America Needs Migrant Farmworkers

Every year, thousands of migrant farmworkers, many like Joel and Diana Villarreal, many very different, travel the highways and back roads of America to labor in the nation's fields and orchards. The course of these human streams is always north, following the ripening crops. After they harvest the vegetables and fruits in Washington, Minnesota, New York, and other states along the Canadian border, the migrant streams turn south toward the places they started from. For some, there will be late crops and second plantings to harvest along the road back. The growing of food in America never stops.

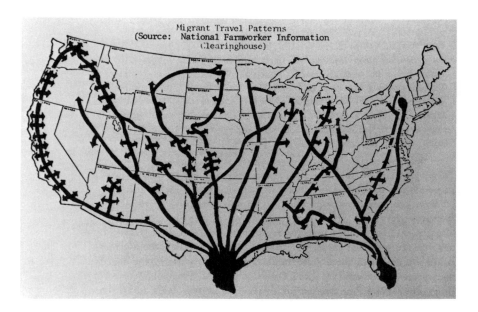

Migrant Travel Patterns
(Source: National Farmworker Information Clearinghouse)

Agriculture is a highly mechanized industry in the United States today. Fields are prepared by tractors pulling plows. Machines plant many crops. Pesticides are sprayed on fields from airplanes. Irrigation systems are automated. The great grain crops are harvested mechanically, as are soybeans, cotton (except on some small farms), and some vegetables and fruits. Trucks carry the bounty of the fields to markets, storage facilities, and processing plants.

Efforts to increase mechanization never cease, but machines have not been invented that can satisfactorily replace human hands in harvesting and preparing for market many of the vegetables and fruits grown in America. Oranges, lemons, and other citrus, apples, strawberries, peaches, pears, asparagus, cucumbers, squash, peppers, tomatoes for the fresh market, lettuce, broccoli, cabbage—those and many more still need care in selection, picking, and handling, which mechanical claws cannot give.

Farming in America today is big business. Since World War II the number of farms in this country has decreased from 6 million to 2.5 million, and the decrease continues by the tens of thousands every year. Thousands of large agricultural companies and giant corporations have entered the farming business by absorbing smaller farms. Individual farm owners have not disappeared, but often they grow crops under contract for such companies as Del Monte, Stokeley-Van Camp, and Minute Maid. Most of these farms and agricultural companies are almost totally dependent on migrant labor to harvest their vegetable and fruit crops and to work in the plants that process them.

According to the U.S. Department of Agriculture, there are about 2.5 million hired seasonal workers who work on farms in the areas where they live but do not migrate—an average of one for every farm in America. They help farm owners in field preparation, planting, crop maintenance, and harvesting. But when a vegetable or fruit crop ripens, it must be picked quickly, in a few days or weeks. It is then that farms must have a large force of harvesters or face disaster. The answer is migrants, who arrive in their jumble of old cars, station wagons, trucks, and secondhand school buses, pick the fruits and vegetables, and move on to the next harvest.

How Many Migrants?

No one knows how many migrants travel throughout America each year harvesting the nation's crops. Twenty years ago, in a bitter book entitled *The Slaves We Rent,* Truman Moore wrote that the United States does a better job of counting its migratory birds than it does counting migrant farmworkers.

In 1985 we still do not have figures that anyone has much confidence in, but we are not likely to get better ones. People constantly on the move are hard to count. Counting the children of migrants who work in the fields beside their parents is even harder. Hardest of all is estimating the number of illegal aliens in the migrant farmworker streams.

A 1976 study by the governor's office in Texas put the number of persons in Texas migrant households at 375,000. An Indiana study in 1975 reported that 184,000 migrants in that state worked on farms or in food-processing plants at some time during the year. Those are probably the most specific figures we have. Two recent studies estimate that the number of migrant farmworkers nationally is about 800,000, plus an unknown number of children who work full time or part time in harvesting crops. Those are only informed guesses, but they are the best figures available.

Who Are Migrant Farmworkers?

Over the decades, many different people have been migrant farmworkers in America. In the late nineteenth century and early part of the twentieth, large numbers of Chinese, Japanese, and

Filipinos were brought from Asia to work on West Coast farms. During the same period, immigrants from Ireland, Italy, and Scandinavia did seasonal agricultural work on the East Coast. Southern blacks and whites were the migrant farmworkers in the South and over time replaced European immigrants in the East. They also were the principal migrants in the Midwest. Mexican-Americans supplied most of the migrant farm labor in the Southwest and much of it in California.

Today the picture is very different. People of Hispanic background—Mexican-Americans, Mexican nationals, Puerto Ricans, Central Americans—make up at least 70 percent of the migrant work force, and the percentage is increasing. Black Americans now comprise only about 15 percent of migrants nationally, and whites less than 10 percent. Another approximately 5 percent is made up of workers from some of the Caribbean islands. A few workers from other parts of the world complete the total.

The decline of blacks as migrants began with increased educational and job opportunities that grew out of the great civil rights revolution of the 1960s, and the decline continues to this day. The case of Melvis Gilliard and her family illustrates what has happened to many—but by no means all—black migrants.

Melvis was one of twelve children in a farmworker family that lived in the small north Florida town of Hastings. From the time she was a child, Melvis worked with her parents and brothers and sisters cutting cabbage, picking beans, and sacking potatoes in the rich fields around Hastings. Every summer, the family traveled to North Carolina and worked there for several months, always for the same farmer.

Melvis married in 1945, and she and her husband continued the same pattern, working on farms around Hastings and going to North Carolina for work in the summer. In time, they had thirteen children.

"And they learned to work in the fields," Melvis told Paul and me.

Melvis Gilliard at the wheel of her Migrant Head Start school bus in Hastings, Florida.

"All of them?" I asked.

"Every last one of them," Melvis said firmly.

There was a difference, however. Melvis's children worked during the summers, but the rest of the time they went to school; and as they grew older, they were able to find work outside of the fields. Today, only one of Melvis's thirteen children remains a migrant farmworker. One daughter is a cook at the Holiday Inn in the nearby town of Palatka; another daughter is a waitress there. One son has made the army a career; one works in a furniture store; another owns a car wash. One daughter is a registered nurse.

But Melvis smiled when she recalled that two of her daughters, married to servicemen in Missouri, came East last year to work the potato season in North Carolina.

"Why?" I asked her.

"Just in their blood, I guess," Melvis said.

Vera Hammond

For some, however, changing times have brought no escape from the migrant life. We met Vera Hammond and her daughter, who is also named Vera, on the porch of a dilapidated shack in Hastings. Eight other people live there. During the late fall and winter, Mrs. Hammond and her daughter cut cabbage in the fields around Hastings. In the spring and summer they travel north to Georgia, South Carolina, and North Carolina to pick tomatoes, sort and sack potatoes, and do any other field work that is available.

"There ain't nothin' good about it," Vera Hammond said, talking about her life as a migrant worker. "You don't never make enough money, no matter how long you work. You nearly faint from the heat. Stripping tobacco plants all day is terrible. So is working on ladders from morning to night with a bucket or bag strapped around you, and it gets heavier the longer you work.

"And contractors," she continued, speaking of men who recruit work crews and take them north. "If there's a good one, I ain't never met him. They keep your money just as long as they can."

Mrs. Hammond has been a migrant farmworker from the time she married thirty years ago, but her parents were not migrants. "They had more sense," she told me.

Vera Hammond's daughter dropped out of school in the ninth grade. She has no thoughts about the future except to continue what she is doing now. "I'll just keep going on the season," she said, "and cuttin' cabbage around here."

Vera Moore

Vera Hammond and her daughter, Vera Moore, pose in front of the shack they live in outside of Hastings, Florida.

Kim Whitfield also lives in Hastings, in a barracks-type building with one-room quarters that rent for sixty dollars a month. There is no water, no bathroom, and no kitchen in the building. Kim is twenty-five and has three children.

One of ten children in a migrant family, Kim has been doing farm work since she was thirteen, and she still goes north to work the crops every year with her father and two or three of her brothers and sisters. She has a high school diploma, but it has not helped her get out of the migrant life. Kim would like to go to a vocational and technical school in nearby St. Augustine.

"It's not far," Kim said, "but it's a long way when you have three kids and no money."

The reason people of Hispanic background are the dominant population in migrant work in the United States today is rooted in geography and economics. The two-thousand-mile border that this country shares with Mexico cannot be effectively policed. Every year hundreds of thousands of Mexicans, half a million by some estimates, cross illegally into the United States to seek work that is not available in Mexico. Large numbers of these illegals, or undocumented persons as they are called by the government, have farm backgrounds or no job skills at all. If they are not caught by the border patrol, they swell the ranks of migrant workers.

The large Mexican-American population of Texas also adds greatly to the Hispanic total in migrant farm work. The Texas study referred to earlier counted over sixty thousand migrant families that travel in the farmworker streams, with parents, children, and in many cases grandparents, engaging in the work of making a living for the family.

Such a family are the Izaguirres, whom we met during the strawberry "digging" season in New York. Victoriano Izaguirre and his wife have been migrant farmworkers since they were

Victoriano Izaguirre, his wife, and a grandchild in Williamson, New York.

children. They have nine daughters and five sons, all of whom have been field workers at some time. Their home is Mercedes, Texas, but they are there for only short periods during the year, to relax and be with friends. The rest of the time they and their children who are still a part of the household are on the road.

"We listen and go where the work is," said Sergio, one of the older sons.

In 1984 their travel took them to Florida from December until March to pick oranges. They returned to Texas for two weeks and then drove to Washington to cut asparagus in April, May, and June. They came back to Texas for another two weeks of rest before going to New York to spend July and August in the onion fields. Tomato picking took them to Virginia in late August and September, and by October they were back in New York working on a big strawberry farm about forty miles from Rochester.

At this time of year, their job, along with other migrants and some local workers, is to prepare strawberry plants for shipment to Florida. The plants are shipped to Florida by the millions in refrigerated trucks. The whole Izaguirre family works in a large processing shed, trimming the freshly dug strawberry plants, gathering them into bunches of twenty-five, and packing forty bunches in a box, making a total of one thousand plants to a box. For every box packed, they are paid $7.50. Working together, the family can make three hundred dollars on a good day. A good day is a day when it does not rain, and when plants are brought from the fields as fast as the packers can handle them.

In New York, the Izaguirres live in a huge old fifteen-room white house, along with about thirty other migrants. Living space in the house is furnished rent free by the owner of the strawberry farm, although each person is charged a dollar a day for electricity. For the Izaguirres, that amounts to $270 a month or more. The Izaguirres have three rooms for the nine persons now in their family group. Waiting their chance to get into the kitchen to cook their meal at night and into the bathroom to take a bath, after

Janie Izaguirre prepares strawberry plants for shipment.

heating water in the kitchen, requires patience and skilled timing. With a nice touch of humor, the strawberry farmworkers call their quarters The White House.

When the Izaguirres are finished with the strawberry plants, they will return to Texas in their Ford panel truck and spend two or three weeks in Mercedes before starting again for Florida to pick oranges. "It's a hard life," said Janie Izaguirre, who still thinks about going back to school, "but we're putting money in the bank for the time there won't be work."

With Florida facing its greatest citrus crisis in years because of the terrible freezes in 1983 and 1985, that time could come soon.

The Crew Leader System

More than anything else, farmers want to be assured of an abundant supply of labor when their fruits and vegetables are ready to be harvested. These are "time critical" crops, and getting them picked when they are at their prime, when the weather is right, and when market conditions are at their best can make the difference between a million-dollar harvest and a financial disaster. In this high-risk, high-gain business, the grower wants to control everything possible, and the way he has found to control his supply of harvest labor—to make sure it is there when he needs it—is through the farm labor contractor, or crew leader as he is usually called.

The estimated eleven thousand crew leaders in America vary widely in their operations and their personal characteristics. Some manage small crews made up of family members and friends; others are responsible for crews of five hundred or more workers. An average-size crew is probably between twenty and thirty workers.

Regardless of the size of the crew, the crew leader has many tasks. He finds growers who need workers and guarantees to supply the necessary number at the time they are needed. He transports the crew to where they are going to work. This may be a few miles, in another part of the state, or halfway across the country. No matter where they are working, he is responsible for getting them to the fields every day. He usually has a bus, perhaps several, and sometimes trucks and loading equipment that the grower requires as a part of the contract. Such crew leaders are owner-businessmen as well as labor recruiters.

The crew leader is manager of the camp where his crew is housed. He usually directs the work in the fields and often is responsible for the whole harvest operation until the produce has been delivered to the packing house. He pays the crew their daily or weekly wages, and sometimes he lends money to crew members or extends them credit for food, clothes, or whiskey. He is responsible for the behavior of his crew in the fields and elsewhere, if they are working away from their home base.

The crew leader makes his money in a number of ways. Sometimes he is paid a certain amount, perhaps fifty dollars, each day he delivers his crew to the fields. He usually will be paid for supervising the crew while they work. He almost always will receive a percentage of whatever his crew earns. If the crew receives thirty-five cents for each bucket of tomatoes picked, the crew leader may receive five cents per bucket from the grower. A crew member who picks two hundred buckets in a day makes seventy dollars for himself and ten dollars for the crew leader. If there are thirty members of the crew who also pick two hundred buckets, the crew leader will make three hundred dollars from their work that day.

From the money he receives, the crew leader must pay for his buses and other equipment, pay transportation costs, and buy insurance. If he is an honest crew leader, he must maintain Social Security records for his crew. Some crew leaders become rich. Others lead a shaky financial existence and go out of business. The same vagaries of weather, market prices, and labor supply that affect growers and migrant farmworkers affect crew leaders.

Almost all crew leaders have spent much of their lives as migrant laborers. They know from long first-hand experience what the life is like. They know and understand the kinds of people who become migrants. They become crew leaders because they are able to save some money or convince someone to give them credit for equipment and other start-up costs.

But more than anything, a crew leader must have the ability to be convincing. He must be able to convince a grower or manager of an agricultural company that he can and will deliver a crew when it is needed and that he can handle the crew once it is working. He must be able to convince migrants that he really has work for them and that they can follow him, sometimes a

Migrants pick and prepare broccoli for the market in the Rio Grande Valley of Texas.

thousand miles or more, with reasonable expectation of being treated fairly. A crew leader may be a good man or a bad man, but he is always a persuasive man.

A successful crew leader must be able to control his crew. Some crew leaders establish their control by fair and prompt pay, by getting to know their workers and having a real concern for their problems, by providing safe transportation, and by trying to secure the best housing available for the crew.

Unfortunately, many crew leaders control their workers by threats and fear, including physical beating of crew members. They furnish food, cigarettes, and whiskey to workers on credit and charge them exorbitant prices so that the workers are always in debt and cannot get away. This method of control is called peonage and is really a form of slavery. In the last five years, scores of crew leaders in various parts of the country have been convicted of peonage by the U.S. Department of Justice civil rights division under nineteenth-century antislavery laws.

Criticism of the crew leader system abounds, but federal and state laws that have been passed to try to curb its abuses have met with limited success. The fact remains that the system is a part of the migrant farmworkers' world and that no end to it is in sight.

Home Bases and Migrant Streams

Three great reservoirs of migrant farmworkers exist in America. The biggest of the three is Texas, with a concentration heavily in the southern part of the state, particularly the Rio Grande Valley. Ninety-five percent of the migrants who live in Texas are of Mexican ancestry; some are U.S. citizens whose parents and grandparents made Texas their home; some are legal alien residents, "green carders" with government approval to work in the United States; others are in the country illegally.

Some of the workers migrate only in Texas, traveling from county to county to pick the vegetable, fruit, and melon crops as they mature. Others leave Texas during the spring and summer to harvest crops throughout the rest of the country. For some, the route leads through New Mexico and Arizona to California and on up the coast to Oregon and Washington. Some go to Ohio and Indiana to pick and process tomatoes; others make their way to Michigan and Minnesota for the fruit harvests. Still others go to Florida during the winter for the citrus and vegetable seasons. There are no harvest fields and orchards in America that some Texas migrants do not visit, but Texas is their home base to which they always return.

The second great reservoir is California, which employs far more farmworkers, both migrants and nonmigrants, than any other state. California has become a true agricultural giant. Its broad river valleys, extensive irrigation systems, and long growing season have made it the leader in cash farm income, producing 40 percent of the country's vegetables and fruits. Some examples: California supplies 70 percent of the nation's lettuce, 65 percent of the tomatoes, 92 percent of the table grapes, 60 percent of the celery, 55 percent of the strawberries, and almost 100 percent of such foods as dates, figs, and olives. Most California migrants spend their time working in different parts of the state, but some go to Oregon and Washington for the apple, strawberry, and other fruit and vegetable harvests.

America's most famous migrant farmworkers, the Joad family in John Steinbeck's novel *The Grapes of Wrath,* left the Oklahoma dust bowl of the Depression era and made their way to California. Many Midwestern farmers migrated to the West Coast during that period, and today some of their sons, daughters, and grandchildren remain there as farmworkers and, in some cases, farm owners. Some children of Filipinos brought to California during the 1920s continue in farm work. The largest number of migrant farmworkers in California, however, are Mexican-Americans who are citizens or legal residents and Mexicans who are illegal aliens.

Harvesting broccoli, with the help of a huge machine-driven con-veyor belt, near Salinas, California.

Migrant worker in California.

The third great reservoir of migrant farmworkers in America is Florida. Florida's vast orange, grapefruit, lemon, lime, and tangerine groves and huge vegetable farms provide work from November to May. During the late spring, summer, and early fall, the migrants move up the Atlantic seaboard harvesting crops from Georgia to New York. By November they have returned to Florida, their home base.

For decades, the migrant farmworkers of Florida were largely blacks who usually were following in their parents' footsteps. Many blacks in Florida continue to work as migrants, but in recent years workers of Hispanic background have replaced them as the majority, not only as workers in Florida but also in the East Coast stream. Many Texas Mexican-Americans have shifted their home base to Florida, while others, mostly illegal aliens, have come directly from Mexico and Central America. A steadily decreasing number of whites in Florida also are migrants.

For years, Florida sugarcane growers have brought workers from Jamaica to harvest that crop; they have done this under a special government "guest worker" program, contending that American workers do not have the skills to cut sugarcane efficiently. More recently, Haitians, fleeing the poverty and political malice of their country, have come to Florida and have joined the East Coast migrant stream.

Some migrant farmworkers live in other states—particularly in the South and Southwest—but Texas, California, and Florida are the home bases in the United States for probably 90 percent of the workers who follow the crops. Mexico remains home for most of the migrants who cross illegally into the United States.

The travel patterns of migrant farmworkers can be called streams only in the sense that there is a general movement toward traditional harvest areas. No person or government agency oversees or manages the streams. A family usually returns to where it has been before, often having an understanding with a farmer from season to season, but, like the Izaguirre family, most "listen

An elderly migrant takes a break in an orange grove in central Florida.

A migrant camp in one of California's central valleys.

and go where the work is," sometimes changing plans in mid-stream. Crew leaders are supposed to have contracts with farms to which they take their workers, but crew leaders, too, can improvise if they hear of good opportunities. Bad weather, early or late harvests, or rumors of a bumper crop somewhere can cause turns in the migrants' road. The streams are meandering ones.

The Migrant Condition

What is life like for most migratory workers? The picture drawn from a number of government and university studies looks like this:

—The average lifespan of a migrant farmworker is forty-nine years, compared to the seventy-four-year lifespan of the average American.

—The infant and maternal death rate for migrant farmworkers is two-and-a-half times higher than the national average.

—Preventable infections and diseases such as tuberculosis, flu, pneumonia, intestinal parasites, and teeth and gum deterioration occur at a 200 to 500 percent higher rate among migrants and their families than among the general population.

—Farm work is hazardous. The disability rate for migratory or seasonal farmworkers is three times that of the general population. Falls from ladders in apple and citrus orchards are common, as are accidents with loaders and other field equipment. Migrants work at a feverish pace because they usually are paid by the amount they pick. They are always fighting fatigue as the workday progresses, particularly the children, and their thoughts are not on safety but on filling buckets and bins.

—Pesticide poisoning is one of the most serious health problems. The U.S. Food and Drug Administration has estimated that as many as one thousand agricultural workers may be killed annually by pesticides and as many as ninety thousand injured.

—Migrant farmworkers are the poorest-paid workers in America. A 1982 study showed that, while the average American family had an income of over $22,000 a year, the median income for a migrant farmworker family of six was about $4,000.

—Child labor is outlawed in every U.S. industry except agriculture. From the age of fourteen, any child can work in the fields without restriction. Any twelve- or thirteen-year-old can work with his parents' consent. A child of *any* age can labor on farms that are not covered by the minimum-wage law, and many are not. A study made for the U.S. Department of Health and Human Services states: "Child labor is an economic necessity for the migrant family due to the low level of income. By the age of four, most children work in the fields at least part of the day. And most older children drop out of school well before high school to work full-time in the fields."

—The figures on school dropouts are grim. Sixty percent of all children of migrant farmworkers will quit school before the ninth grade. Only about 11 percent will enter the twelfth grade.

—Housing for migrant farmworkers has traditionally been wretched. Some of the big agricultural companies—especially on the West Coast—now provide modern, improved quarters or trailers, but overall housing for migrants is still very bad. Following is a statement about migrant housing by a public health doctor testifying at a congressional hearing: "We saw housing and living conditions horrible and dehumanizing to the point of disbelief . . . without heat, adequate light or ventilation, and containing no plumbing or refrigeration. Each room (no larger than eight by fourteen feet) is the living space for an entire family, approximately suggesting slave quarters of earlier days. . . ."

The injustice that migrant farmworkers suffer in America was summed up eloquently by Dr. Robert Coles, a distinguished psychiatrist who has done much work with migrant children. Testifying before a Senate subcommittee on migratory labor in 1969, Dr. Coles said:

No group of people I have worked with—in the South, in Appalachia, and in our northern ghettoes—tries harder to work, indeed travels all over the country working, working from sunrise to sunset, seven days a week when the crops are there to be harvested.

There is something ironic and special about that, too. In exchange for the desire to work, for the terribly hard work of bending and stooping to harvest our food, these workers are kept apart like no others, denied rights and privileges no others are denied, denied even halfway decent wages, asked to live homeless and vagabond lives, lives of virtual peonage.

Despite some improvement in help for migrant children and better housing here and there, the conditions that Dr. Coles described in 1969 are largely unchanged today and in some ways even worse.

3
Migrant Families
in the Streams

A migrant enjoys a seasonal respite in La Grulla, Texas.

F AMILIES FORM a permanent core of migrant labor in America. Single migrants drift in and out of farm work and find other ways to make a living, but third generation migrant families are common. No fondness for the migrant life keeps them moving in the streams year after year. They are there because harvesting crops is what they know how to do, what they have done from the time they were children. Few members of migrant families have had many years of schooling because they were needed in the fields to help the family survive. Their education was in the bean and tomato fields, the grape vineyards, the citrus orchards.

In south Texas, a deep attachment to their traditional home keeps many Mexican-American families in migrant work. It is splendid country. The Rio Grande Valley is fertile, crops abundant and food cheap, the winters usually short and mild. The heritage of their ancestors is in this immense valley which was once a part of Mexico. It is truly their homeland.

Rafael Guerra, who works for the Texas Migrant Council in Rio Grande City, Texas.

Many families can find work picking Texas oranges and Ruby Red grapefruit, broccoli, cucumbers, peppers, melons, and numerous other crops. Even so, the economy of the Valley is always depressed, an economy poorer than Appalachia's. The number of agricultural workers is so great, and the border is so easy for illegal workers from Mexico to cross, that many families must migrate to find enough work to stay alive.

Rafael Guerra was a third-generation migrant who spent most of his youth in the fields until he broke out of the cycle by going to school. Now he works for the Texas Migrant Council, which sponsors migrant development programs, and he knows the problems of the area very well.

"There is always someone from across the river who will work for less," Guerra told Paul.

Some families might escape the migrant life if they moved permanently from south Texas, but few will do that. Hector and Angelica Castillo, who live in San Benito in the Valley, are an example of this reluctance; their situation is much like that of Joel and Diana Villarreal. Hector and Angelica were born in the Rio Grande Valley. Their parents were migrants, but Hector was able to complete his training as a mechanic and, when he and Angelica married, to find work in construction projects. They began making payments on a trailer home, and they looked forward to a life in San Benito. But in too short a time, Hector's jobs as a mechanic came to an end, and they made the hard decision to go back into migrant work.

In 1981 they signed with a farm labor contractor to work in Alabama and Indiana. The work has been steady in both places and the pay slightly above minimum wage, so they have continued to go there every year since their trial journey. They leave San Benito in April with their two preschool-age daughters and return in October. They have a compact car, so they cannot carry many of their belongings. Fortunately, there are Migrant Head Start programs in the places they work, so the children have good care.

In Alabama, Angelica sorts potatoes all day, six or seven days a week, picking out those that are rotten, green, or malformed, also looking for rocks, toads, and anything else that shouldn't be in the river of potatoes that flows through the sorting machine. Hector sews the sacks of potatoes and sometimes loads them onto a trailer. They live in one room in a workers' barracks, but their room does have a tiny stove and refrigerator. Portable toilets are outside, as is the camp's only shower.

After Alabama, they go to Geneva, Indiana, and their living quarters there are much better. They have a trailer with a kitchen and bathroom all to themselves. But their work schedule is frightening. Hector works from seven in the morning until seven at night packing boxes, with an eighteen-minute break for lunch. Angelica sorts tomatoes from five o'clock in the evening until five in the morning. They work six or seven days a week and hardly see each other, or the children, for the weeks that they are there.

Angelica says plant officials have told her that they cannot find many local people who will work the long hours that the short, frantic tomato season requires. More and more, they depend on Hispanics from Texas and Florida. But Hector and Angelica do not complain about the schedule.

"We have come to work," she said to me, while they were still at the Indiana plant.

"Have you ever thought about moving from south Texas?" I asked. "Going to live someplace where Hector might find steady work as a mechanic?"

Angelica looked at me in surprise. "No," she said. "San Benito is our home."

A Home in Texas

It is probable that this sense of place, of needing a place to call home, of having a home to return to, is stronger in people who live or have lived the migrant life than in any other group of people. Every migrant—there is no exception—has his or her share of bitter memories of life on the road, memories that never dim, that make a home, no matter how modest, a treasure without equal.

Rafael Guerra has vivid memories of his many trips north from his home in the Rio Grande Valley. He described some of them to Paul. "Fifty people with wooden suitcases would be packed into an open truck equipped with double gas tanks. There would be enough gas to reach the Texas Panhandle without stopping, and there we would have one five-minute break. Once we were away from Texas, the workers would be stuck—no money, no way to get home—and we would be at the mercy of the crew chiefs. Some of them were cruel men.

"We lived in terrible places when we were working in the fields, sometimes chicken coops, really. No windows, no plumbing, no water, swarms of mosquitoes every night in some places. The walls were like paper, and you could hear everything, babies crying all night. My mother used to douse the floors with kerosene where we stayed, to kill the bugs. Mother would make us clean a place spotlessly the day before we left. She wanted people to know that we didn't live that way at home."

Paul met Francisco Lumbreras in Edinburg, another Rio Grande Valley town. Francisco has lived there since he was four years old. One of fourteen children in a migrant family, he too has memories of migrant life that have not faded. "Housing was terrible when we were on the road," he said. "I can remember a place in West Texas where we were picking cotton. We lived in an old cotton gin for four weeks. We could hear the wind whistling through, and it was cold.

"When we got back to Edinburg in the late fall each year, we would walk seven miles to the Virgin of San Juan to say thank you for protecting us on the road. Migrants still do that."

Francisco now teaches fourth grade at Edinburg's Travis Elementary School, which he attended as a child. Many of his pupils

Teacher Francisco Lumbreras and his fourth grade class in Edinburg, Texas.

are migrant children. "I stayed in Edinburg because of them," he told Paul. "I could have gone someplace else after college, but I knew this is where I should be."

Francisco gives credit to his parents for helping him break out of the migrant life. "They made education the number-one priority. Even if we lived someplace only a month, they didn't waste a day getting us enrolled. There were times I would go to four or five schools in one year. It was hard because there were always new teachers and books and kids. I learned to get along with all sorts of people; maybe that was good, at least. But so many kids suffer from being pulled around to different schools like that. I can remember eighteen-year-olds in the seventh grade.

"I know one teacher can make a difference. It did for me. When I was in the ninth grade, I had a teacher, Mr. Sandoval, who had been a migrant when he was a boy. He had gone on and got a college degree, and he made me believe that I could do the same thing."

But Francisco knows how hard it can be for a migrant child. "Ninety percent of them are hurt by the constant moving around," he said. "Out of a class of forty-five migrant children I was in during elementary school, only five graduated from high school, and only two went to college. I was one of them."

Estela Rodriguez is Francisco's sister. She now lives in Haines City, Florida, with her husband Domingo and their three sons. Estela and Domingo first met when they were in the third grade in Edinburg; both their families were migrants traveling different roads, so over the years they saw each other only during a few winter months. But in time they married and made their way to the orange groves of Florida as pickers. They have stayed there and today have a comfortable home in Haines City. Domingo is a crew leader in the citrus groves from November to June and hauls tomatoes in Indiana with a small fleet of his own trucks during the summer and early fall. They have made the change from south Texas to Florida as more and more migrants have, but Edinburg and the Rio Grande Valley remain very much a part of their lives.

By chance, I met Estela in Haines City before Paul met Francisco in Edinburg. "I came with my family to Edinburg when I was eight years old," Estela told me. "We came from Mexico and we came legally. It took my father years to get the approvals. We rented a house in Edinburg, and we became farmworkers in the Valley and many other places. We picked cotton in West Texas. We picked strawberries, cherries, blueberries, blackberries in Oregon and Washington. We sacked potatoes in Idaho.

"All of the children worked. I started in the fields when I was eight years old. But we went to school, too. We worked in the summers and on weekends and other times when there was no

Estela and Domingo Rodriguez and two of their sons.

school. Everyone worked in the fields except my mother. My father said that she was needed at home, to make a home for the family, and that is what she did. No matter where we were or what kind of a place we lived in, we had a home.

"As soon as he could, my father bought a house in Edinburg. It was not a very big house, and we had to make mortgage payments on it, of course, but it belonged to our family, and it was always there for us to come back to."

The family has built a new house there now, on the same spot as the old one. Mr. Lumbreras, the father, lives in it, now retired from work in the fields. The house remains a refuge for members of the family when they are in need. A few years after Estela and

Domingo went to Florida, he was badly hurt in a truck accident. They returned to Edinburg and lived in the house during his slow recovery, helped by other members of the family.

Most of the Lumbreras children now live in other parts of the country; in some cases they have made homes in places where they worked as a migrant family, Oregon and Idaho. Several still are in food processing or farming, but most are doing other work.

Several members of the family continue to live in Edinburg. Two besides Francisco are teachers. One of them, Belisario, also teaches the fourth grade at Travis Elementary. When Estela talks about this brother, her eyes shine.

"Belisario started school in Mexico, before we ever came to Texas," she said. "When he was in the eighth grade in Edinburg, he was kicked out of school. Yes, kicked out. I think it was for arguing too much with a teacher about how the history of Mexico was taught in Edinburg. Anyway, he went to work full time in the fields after that. Then he was drafted and went to Vietnam. In Vietnam, Belisario decided to get his high school diploma through an army study program, and he did. When he got back from Vietnam, he got a job driving a truck, but then Francisco convinced him that he should go to college. Now he is teaching school, like Francisco.

"I used to say to Belisario, 'Whenever I think I can't do something, I think about you. Then I think I can do it.' "

Estela has done a great deal. She quit school when she married Domingo, but later she got her high school diploma through an adult study program. She studied bookkeeping and typing at a vocational training center in Haines City so that she could help Domingo with his work.

For the past eight years, Estela has worked with the East Coast Migrant Head Start Project. She began as a bus aid, helping the bus driver get the young migrant children to the day-care center and home safely. In time, she became director of a center, and now she is in the project headquarters in Haines City helping

This cheerful youngster attends a day-care center for migrant children in Haines City, Florida.

to monitor migrant child-care centers and programs throughout Florida.

When I asked Estela about the dark side of migrant life, she talked about the familiar things: the poor pay, the specter of no work, the constant moving from place to place, the bleak housing. "Is there any satisfaction in the migrant life?" I asked.

Estela reflected for a moment. "It is honest work," she replied. "I tell migrant children to be proud of their parents for that."

Recently the Lumbreras family held a reunion in Edinburg. There were other places with bigger houses where they could have held it, but they all wanted to come back to their home in Texas.

Being Poor

To be a migrant is to be poor. You may pick three hundred buckets of tomatoes one day and make a hundred dollars, and for the next two days it rains and you make nothing. You stay in the Rio Grande Valley to pick grapefruit during the winter season, but a sudden cold front freezes the fruit on the trees, and there is no work. You are on your way to the raspberry harvest in Michigan when your car breaks down. When you arrive three days late, the jobs are all taken. You finally find work in Minnesota, but the house you thought you could rent for two hundred dollars a month costs five hundred. There is always something to keep a migrant poor.

Migrant families that fight their way to a level a little above poverty usually do so at the cost of their children's education and often their health. If everyone works, the family may be just a little less poor.

That is the way it was for Oralia Leal's family. Her name was Oralia Gutierrez then, when she was a child, but everyone called her Lali. The Gutierrez family were migrants in the truest sense. They followed the crops ten or eleven months a year and over the years traveled throughout much of the southwestern and eastern parts of the country. Lali remembers hoeing and picking cotton in Oklahoma, picking cherries in Michigan, bell peppers and cucumbers in North Carolina and Virginia, tomatoes in Pennsylvania, and sacking potatoes in Alabama.

"I started picking cotton when I was ten years old," Lali told us. "I pulled a regular-size sack fourteen feet long, and I could pick as much as almost anyone. We started picking in the morning and didn't stop until it was dark. When we started cleaning cotton in the summer—hoeing weeds—it was so hot you thought you would melt. When we finished picking in the fall, some days it was so cold my fingers were numb. I guess I liked picking peppers best. You could fill a bucket and it wasn't so heavy.

"We traveled in a truck with a canvas tarpaulin over the back.

Farmworker's house in the lower Rio Grande Valley.

Oralia Leal with her parents in Immokalee, Florida. Behind them on the wall is a wedding photograph of Oralia's grandparents.

The kids all rode back there with the bedding, food, pots and pans, and clothes. My clothes were always packed in a box. I never had a suitcase.

"If the farm we worked on didn't have housing, we would have to find a place to live. Sometimes it would take a week or two to find a house, and we would just live in the truck. My mother would build a fire and cook our meals beside the truck.

"There was never enough money. Sometimes we didn't get paid nearly as much as my father thought we were going to get.

Sometimes we didn't have money for clothes or even food, and my mother would go to the church for help. But she didn't do that unless she really had to. She always bought our clothes at yard sales.

"I went to school a little bit but not much, maybe two months a year. My parents knew it was important, but the money I could make in the fields when we had a chance to work was more important. I couldn't get much out of school anyway because I didn't speak any English then, just Spanish.

"It was a hard life, but there were good things about it, too. The family was always together, and we usually traveled with five or six other families, so we were with people we knew. We were all poor, so we were all the same. And we could still have good times together.

"Sometimes on a Saturday, we would not work or stop work early. We would go to town crowded in the back of a truck, maybe twenty or thirty young men and women, to buy food and clothes and just have a good time. If there was money, my father would give us each a dollar. We would eat ice cream and go to a Western movie.

"Sometimes someone asks me if I was envious of people I saw in towns who had good homes and good clothes and big new cars. No, I wasn't. They belonged to another world, a world I didn't know anything about. But there was one thing from that world that I did want. I loved music and I always wanted a record player. I used to look at them in the stores, but, of course, I was never able to buy one."

Today Lali lives in Immokalee, Florida. Her husband is a crew leader, and she works for the Redlands Christian Migrant Association. Her job is to persuade migrant parents to put their children in day-care centers run by the Association and to use the centers in learning how to take better care of their children. She has a perfect background for the work and is good at it. The job does not require academic skills, but Lali wants to improve her reading

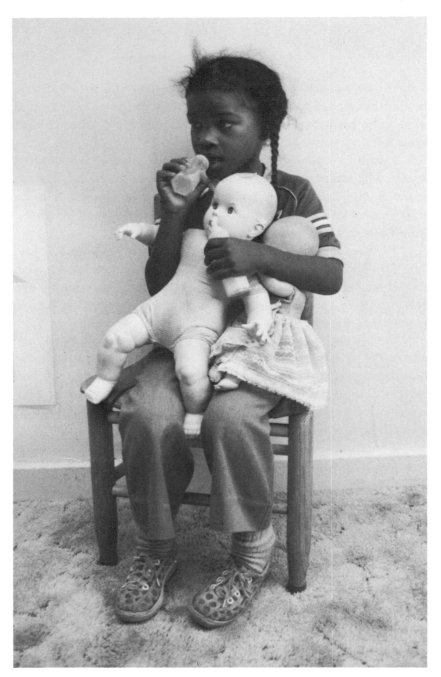

A migrant child with her dolls.

and writing in English. She goes to adult education classes two hours every day.

Most of Lali's family now live in Immokalee. Some still work as migrants. Lali is most proud of her daughter who is in high school and her son who is in college. She is also proud, but in a different way, of her house, her television set, and her record player.

A Friendship in California

Many migrant families work for the same grower year after year. The arrangement benefits everyone. The grower can count on reliable help at harvest time. The migrant family can count on work and does not have to deal with a crew leader. Families with such arrangements have the best chance among migrants of some financial stability and better living conditions, both at their home base and on the road. These long-term relationships sometimes lead to understandings and even friendships that otherwise are unknown between migrants and the people they work for.

Maria Jimenez's father had such an arrangement with a grower in California. "My father was first a bracero," she said to us. "He went to California every year by himself to work, leaving our family in Mexico."

The bracero program started during World War II when the United States was desperately short of farm and railroad labor because of young men going into the armed forces. The U.S. and Mexican governments signed an agreement calling for hundreds of thousands of men from Mexico to work on U.S. farms on a temporary basis. Bracero comes from the word *brazo* (arm); the workers from Mexico were braceros, strong-armed men. U.S. growers liked the program so much (it provided them with inexpensive and steady labor) that the government extended it long after the war. It finally ended in 1964 but only because of pressure from U.S. labor unions.

This is the story Maria told us:

"When my father was a bracero, he always worked for the same grower, and they got along well. When the bracero program ended, my father was able to get approval to keep coming to the United States to work, and he was permitted to bring his family. The man he had worked for during the bracero years wanted him to come back. So in 1967 the whole family went to California, and we went every year after that. We would go in May and come back in October. We traveled in a truck, and it took us three days to get from our home in Acámbaro, Mexico, to Yuba City in northern California. The grower's farm—they call it a ranch in California—was near there.

"I was thirteen when we made our first trip as a family. Four of the children were old enough to work then, along with our father and mother, and I was one of them. The grower's ranch was planted all in peach trees. When we first arrived, we trimmed the trees and cut the shoots that are called suckers. After that we picked peaches for about two months. The bags were heavy when they were full, and you had to be careful not to bruise the peaches when you emptied the bag into the bin. But I learned to be a good peach picker, and I still am today.

"On our way back to Mexico, after the peach season, we would pick olives and oranges in the groves around the town of Porterville—that is not far from Bakersfield. It is wonderful farming country around Porterville, and my father sometimes said he would like to live there someday.

"The owner of the peach ranch, the grower, was an Indian. Not an American Indian but from India. Well, I do not know if he was from India or the West Indies in the Caribbean, but he was an Indian. I am not sure how he and my father became friends, but they were. When he was a bracero, my father would sometimes telephone my mother in Mexico. The grower would let my father use the phone in his house, and he would never charge him for the call. My father had a large family in Mexico. Besides us,

Maria S. Carranza Jimenez and her daughter. They live in Haines City, Florida.

his own family, he had his mother and father and many brothers and sisters. Sometimes my father needed money to help them, and the grower would lend him as much as he needed. They would not sign any paper. The grower would just say, 'Pay me back when you can,' and my father always would.

"There were times the grower had money problems, too. One season when we were there, he did not have money to pay his pickers, and they left. Of course, you cannot blame them. They had no money to live on if they were not paid. But we stayed and picked the peaches. The grower saw that we had food, and we lived in a little house that he furnished us.

"Another time my mother fell from a ladder in the peach orchard and was injured. Lawyers came to my father and told him he could bring a big damage suit against the grower. They said that he and my mother might get a great deal of money, that the grower might have to sell his ranch to pay the judgment. But my father and mother would not listen to them. They would not hurt their friend."

Maria now lives in Florida with her husband and three children. Her husband works in citrus, and on weekends Maria and the twins, who are twelve, join him in picking. In June every year, they pack their car and make the long drive across the country to California. Their first stop in California is Porterville, where Maria's father and mother now live in a house that they own. Her father's dream of living in this wonderful farming country has come true, although he still works part of the year for his old friend near Yuba City.

After a few days' rest in Porterville, Maria and her husband and children drive on to Yuba City. It is peach-picking time, and they will spend the season on the ranch where Maria picked as a young girl. When the peaches are picked, they will go back to Porterville and pick olives until it is time to return to Florida and put the twins in school for the fall term.

Growing Up: A Migrant Childhood

The experiences of a migrant childhood bear little resemblance to those of most other American children. In some ways migrant children grow up faster; they must, to help their families survive. But their hopes, fears, dreams, and desires are those of children everywhere. Juan Medina told us what growing up was like for him.

"I was born in Plainview, Texas. Because I was born in the United States, I was an American citizen. That is the law. But my parents were in the United States illegally. They had slipped

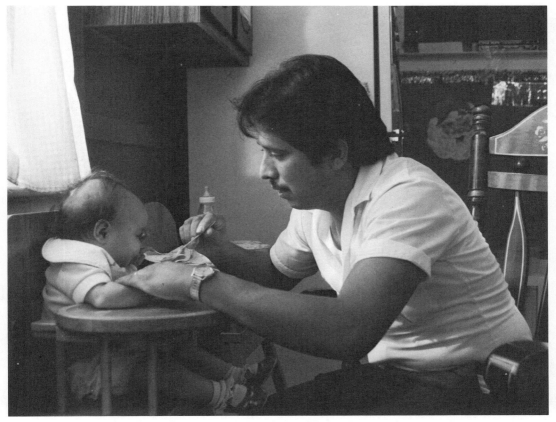

Juan Medina, director of the child-care center in Nocatee, Florida, feeds one of his young charges.

across the border from Mexico to do farm work in Texas because my father could not find a job in Mexico. Two weeks after I was born, my parents were caught by immigration officers and deported to Mexico. I, their U.S. citizen son, was deported with them.

"We went to live with my grandparents in San Pedro, Coahuilla State, Mexico. My parents had three daughters born to them while we were there, and each died while still an infant. I was also a very sickly child, many times on the edge of death, I am told. My grandfather spent much money trying to make me well, money he could not afford, but nothing seemed to help. At last my mother made a promise to the Virgin of San Juan that, if I could be cured, she would take a lock of my hair to the Cathedral of San Juan de las Lagos, a long way from San Pedro. Soon after that I became well, and my mother made her pilgrimage.

"When I was about four years old, my father left again for the United States, this time by himself. We heard about him a few times, but he never returned to our family. After some time my grandparents also crossed the border to work again because they had spent so much money trying to make me well. They were green carders, that is, they had approval to work in the United States. My mother was still an illegal alien, but we went with them because there was nothing else for us to do.

"We went to Colorado where an uncle of mine was a crew leader working for a sugar beet grower. My mother started hoeing in the fields, and it was there that she met the man who became my stepfather.

"I started hoeing sugar beets when I was eight years old. It is hard work, ten hours a day or more, with the sun beating down on you and the hoe handle blistering your hands. What you're doing is cleaning out the weeds, but it is hard to tell weeds from the beet leaves sometimes, so you have to pay attention. You can't just let your mind go blank. You look down the rows, and they're a mile long.

"I started to school in Colorado when I was eight years old, too. My mother made up her mind that I was going to get an education, and my stepfather never stood in the way of that. Sometimes I would have to stay out of school and work because the family had to have more money, but that didn't happen often.

"It was in Colorado that I met Eddie. He was the owner's son on the farm where we lived and worked. I was the only boy on the farm his age, and after school we would play together. I was just a worker's son, but I was welcome in their house, and sometimes I had meals with Eddie and his family. They helped me with my English and that helped me in school, because I spoke mostly Spanish then.

"I had never been in a house like theirs before. It was beautiful, and I never forgot it. Eddie had his own room—I couldn't imagine anything like that—and it was full of toys. They had a big television set in the family room. But what I always thought of most was the inside bathrooms. I had never lived in a house or workers' barracks that had one. I guess everyone has something he is afraid of or hates to do. I hated to go out in the dark to use outside toilets. I was afraid I would step on a snake, and I was afraid of things I couldn't even name. I hated to go out when it was raining and cold.

"I knew one thing. Someday I would have a house like Eddie's, maybe not a big one like his, but it would have an inside bathroom.

"A migrant child learns about responsibility early, and I don't mean just working in the fields. By the time I was ten, my mother and stepfather had two children of their own, two boys. When I wasn't going to school or working, I took care of my brothers and kept the house clean and cooked beans for supper.

"But I was a good worker in the fields. I could fill a hundred sacks of potatoes in the morning and another hundred in the afternoon. We got five cents for every sack filled, so I could make ten dollars for my family on the days I worked. I hated planting onions, though. It was backbreaking work. You had to drag a sack of onion plants down the row and get right down to the ground to make a hole for the plant with your thumb, and sometimes that early in the year the ground was cold and hard, no matter that it had been plowed. You had to put the plants about three inches apart. Sometimes I thought I never would get to the end of a row.

"At first we had to ride in trucks and buses when we were going to some new place with a crew, but little by little my stepfather did better. Finally, he was able to buy his own truck. I was driving it by the time I was fourteen. Besides picking, we could sometimes make money hauling produce from the fields.

"We lived and worked in lots of places—Colorado, Okla-homa, Texas, Alabama, Florida—but my stepfather was born in Texas, and we came to think of Hereford, Texas, in the Panhan-dle, as our home town. After a while we divided our year mainly between Florida and Texas, harvesting cucumbers, tomatoes, squash, and other vegetables in Florida from about October to May and onions, carrots, and potatoes around Hereford in the summer and fall.

"With all this moving around, I never stopped going to school. I don't know if I could name all the places I went, but there was Gilton, Eaton, and Ft. Collins in Colorado and several different schools in Hereford. In Florida I went to Homestead, Bradenton, Tampa, and Ft. Myers. If school was on, I would enroll just as soon as we got to a new work place.

"Some schools I liked and made good friends, but I knew I would have to leave soon, and that was a bad feeling. When my mother told me to bring my report card home, I knew we would be on our way the next day, and sometimes I would have a lump in my throat. Once when we were leaving, my class gave me a going-away party. That night my stepfather said we weren't leaving after all because there was more work. I told him we had to leave because I had had a going-away party. But, of course, we didn't, and I had to go back to school the next day. I was really embarrassed.

"All the years I was growing up, my mother was still an illegal alien. Sometimes when we were living in migrant labor camps, immigration officers would make surprise raids. Those were the worst times of my life. I was so scared I couldn't talk. If my mother had been caught, she would have been sent back to Mex-ico. They don't care if they break up a family. They say the law is the law and has to be enforced.

"My mother had learned to speak English, and that helped her. More than once, the immigration officers would ask her to go around the camp with them and interpret for them. She never got caught, but by the time the immigration people left camp, my mother and I both would be wet with sweat. She has her legal papers now, thank goodness.

"My stepfather left our family twice while I was growing up. He came back after a while the first time, but he left for good the second time. That kind of thing happens pretty often in migrant families, the man just walking out. It's a hard life and they get discouraged and tired of being poor. They just can't take it anymore, and they don't think about their wife who can't walk out. The man thinks it will be different and better if he starts over, but it won't be as long as he's a migrant.

"I was sad when my stepfather left us, but I think maybe I understood his leaving better than my younger brothers did. I never could bring myself to hate him.

"But the first time he left was especially bad. It was winter, and we were living in a migrant camp outside of Hereford, just one room that we could barely keep warm and no plumbing in the building. My mother was pregnant. I don't think we could have made it except for an uncle who helped us. He had his own money problems, but he was a crew leader, and he found work for me. When spring planting time came, I worked extra hard so we could put away enough money for my mother to have her baby in a hospital in Hereford. I was twelve years old that year.

"My mother had her baby in July. She couldn't get into a hospital in Hereford, but I don't know why. My uncle's wife drove her to the little town of Dimmitt about twenty miles away, and she got into a hospital there just barely in time. She had a little girl, and I had a sister. She has always been special to me. Maybe it's because I helped pay for her.

"After my stepfather came back—that is, before he left for good—we got to doing well enough that we were able to buy a house in Hereford. It had an inside bathroom. I'll never forget the first time I walked into that house and knew it was ours. I'm not ashamed to say it. I cried.

"In my junior year at Cypress Lake High School in Ft. Myers,

I enrolled in the local chapter of the Distributive Education Clubs of America. The organization has district and state officers, and the kids in my chapter wanted me to run for Vice President of the Sun District. I said I couldn't do it. There was no way I could get up in front of kids from all over the district and make a speech asking them to nominate me.

"But I had a teacher who told me I could do it. He had taught lots of migrant kids and he knew all about their self-doubts and shyness. He knew how to talk so I could understand him.

" 'Juan,' he told me, 'you can't go through your whole life with your head down.'

"I knew what he meant. That's what a field crop migrant does. He's a stoop laborer. He spends all his life looking down at the ground. Well, I made that speech and I got elected.

"In 1973 I graduated from Cypress Lake High, and I had my head up."

4

Helping Migrant Children:
Hope for Tomorrow

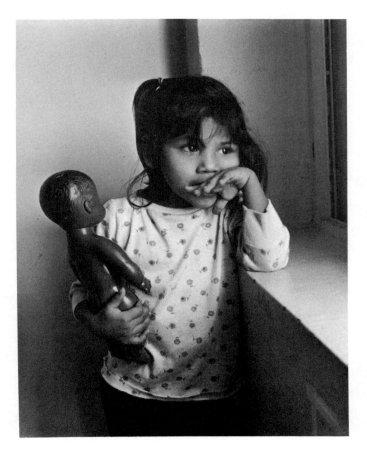

Migrant children learn in a Head Start program at Marion, a crossroads on Maryland's Eastern Shore.

TWELVE YEARS after his graduation from high school, Juan Medina is director of a day-care center for migrant children in Nocatee. The establishment of such centers is one of the few bright spots in the migrant world. And the careful selection of some staff members who have lived and worked as migrants—people like Estela Rodriguez, Oralia Leal, and Juan Medina—shows a rare wisdom on the part of the administrators of migrant child-care programs.

Such an administrator is Sister Geraldine O'Brien, director of the East Coast Migrant Head Start Project, which supervises forty migrant child-care centers from Florida to New York. "We can provide professional help with curriculum, staff training, and financial record keeping," Sister Geraldine said the first time I met her in the Project's small but bustling headquarters in Arlington, Virginia. "What our migrant staff members can provide is an understanding of the children and their parents that can make the difference between the program's success and failure."

"How do you select migrants or former migrants for the staff?" I asked her.

"We look carefully at their backgrounds, of course," Sister Geraldine said, "and we have a migrant parents' committee that screens all prospective staff members, migrant and nonmigrant. They have an instinctive feeling for people who are warm and understanding and genuinely concerned about their children. Sometimes they will go through a list of candidates and not recommend anyone." Sister Geraldine paused a moment. "And there is the providence of God. I believe He is on our selection committees, too."

While they were driving through the Rio Grande Valley, Rafael Guerra, whose job with the Texas Migrant Council is bilingual education, talked to Paul about the days before migrant child-care centers. "Babies and small children were usually taken to the fields," he said. "They were placed by the side of the field or they followed along behind their mothers down the rows. Sometimes they were run over by trucks, even bitten by snakes. They breathed pesticides from the time they were a few weeks old. When I was a baby, I was taken care of in camp by my two-year-old sister."

The Texas Migrant Council runs forty-five day-care centers throughout the state, mostly in the south, and about fifty-five hundred children are enrolled. The Council, or the TMC as everyone calls it, has a unique program for giving continued care to at least some of the preschool migrant children in its Texas centers. When large numbers of migrants move north in the spring, some of the Texas day-care center staffs pack up their equipment, get on buses, and move with them. They set up centers in the Midwestern and Northern states with large numbers of migrants and continue to take care of many of the same migrant children who were in the Texas centers. They know the problems and special needs of these children and can help them better than anyone else.

A youngster gets his first taste of arithmetic.

TMC now runs child-care centers in Washington, Wisconsin, Indiana, Ohio, and Tennessee. The staff members, many of whom were once migrant field workers, are still migrants, but now they are educational migrants. Diana and Joel Villarreal's daughter goes to a special TMC center in Washington, and Angelica and Hector Castillo's children go to one in Indiana.

Instead of moving staff from one location to another as TMC does, the East Coast Migrant Head Start Project moves the children's records. When children leave a Head Start center, their families are given a continuity record for each child that shows his or her health status and learning accomplishments. If a child goes from a Head Start center in Homestead, Florida, and enters another center in Lyons, Georgia, his records will arrive with him. In case the family has lost them, headquarters in Arlington keeps a complete record on every child who has been in any center, and a duplicate set can be forwarded to the new center the child has entered. These records are also of great value when a migrant child enters public school.

In Immokalee, Paul and I visited one of the many child-care centers that the Redlands Christian Migrant Association runs in Florida. The director is Irma Chappa, who spent much of her life as a migrant farmworker.

"My parents were migrants," she told us. "When my brothers and sisters and I were very young, we would go to the field with them in our car early in the morning. We would sit in the car all day until they were through working that night. It was against the law for children to be in the fields or around them, and some growers were afraid they would be fined if the workers' children were seen outside the cars. It was terribly hot even with the windows down, and there was nothing to do but sit. When my mother and father came back to the car for a few minutes for lunch, then we would get out, but that was the only time. There were many children sitting in cars like that."

Now Irma spends her days supervising migrant children play-

Migrant children rehearse a Christmas play in the Head Start school in Nocatee, Florida.

ing with toys, having a good breakfast and lunch, taking a nap in a comfortable bed or crib, riding tricycles, and climbing on the jungle gym on the lawn behind the center.

"It's a very different world from the one you knew," I said to Irma as we watched the children playing.

"And so much better," Irma said.

No matter where they are located, migrant child-care centers have very similar programs. The children are divided into three groups—infants, toddlers, and preschool—and special staff members help each group. Sometimes infants no more than two weeks old are sent to the centers. Toys are plentiful for the different age groups, and babies' cribs often have colorful mobiles hanging above them. The children get two and sometimes three well-balanced meals or snacks during the day.

The days are long. The children are usually at the center by seven in the morning, having been picked up by buses at workers' camps or where migrant houses are clustered. They stay until late in the afternoon, their departure being timed with the arrival of their parents back from the fields. The days are even longer for the staff, who must be at the center before the children arrive and must stay after they leave to get ready for the next day.

The centers are sometimes in church basements, sometimes in schools or public buildings no longer in use—anywhere the organization sponsoring the center can find. But a center must not be cramped and it must be safe. It is always made cheerful with pictures on the walls—some drawn by the preschoolers—and by toys and perhaps a television set and record player.

One goal is to make the children happy and comfortable during their long day's stay, but the center has many other goals. There are educational activities with games, puzzles, building blocks, art, and stories, all of which add up to a quality child development program. The health of each child is a prime concern. Basic health habits like washing hands and brushing teeth are taught, and limited medical, dental, and mental health services are arranged for in the community.

One of the most important objectives of every center is to encourage parents to do as much as possible in the development of their own children. This is done by outreach workers who go to the migrant camps and houses with practical information about nutrition and ways to improve sanitation even in the hardship conditions in which most migrants live. Parents are made aware of community services—health clinics, legal aid, supple-

Head Start youngsters and their teacher in upper New York State.

A migrant mother and her son on Maryland's Eastern Shore.

mentary food centers—that they often do not know about. They are encouraged to visit the day-care centers and to help in volunteer activities, which are also learning experiences for them.

Day-care centers for migrant children are not a new idea. The Mennonites in Florida set up day-care centers in migrant camps as long as forty years ago. The Redlands Christian Migrant Association has run centers since 1965. Many churches or church organizations—the Virginia Council of Churches, the Disciples of Christ, and a number of Catholic parishes, to name only some— have had programs and centers for young migrant children for three decades or more.

But funds made available when Congress passed legislation for the Head Start Program in 1964 made possible a great increase in child-care centers for migrants. Today, all states where migrants work have Migrant Head Start programs. California, with its large migrant population, has seven different organizations that sponsor Head Start child-care centers, such organizations as Campesinos Unidos and Tri-County Migrant Head Start in Fresno.

But there still are not enough centers, not nearly enough, and most of those that do exist do not have space and staff for all who want to come. States with heavy concentrations of migrants during the winter months have the greatest shortages. The Migrant Head Start Center in Belle Glade, Florida, can take care of one hundred children. The waiting list has four hundred names on it. That is the worst, but every other Migrant Head Start center in the state has a waiting list. About nineteen thousand children were enrolled in Migrant Head Start centers in 1984. Probably there was no center or no space available for another fifty thousand migrant children across the country.

I talked to Sister Geraldine about the problem. "Money is the problem," she said. "If we could get a bigger budget from the Department of Health and Human Services, we could start more centers and expand the ones we have now."

"Do you expect more money next year?" I asked.

"Right now it seems that our budget is going to be frozen at the amount we received this year," she said.

"With inflation, that means you won't be able to take care of as many children next year as you have this year," I said.

Sister Geraldine and I were talking on the phone, but I could picture the look of determination on her face, a look I have seen several times before, when she said, "We won't cut back. We'll raise the money somehow."

On a very hot day in August, Paul and I drove to Somerset County on the Eastern Shore of Maryland for the windup of the tomato harvest. We wanted to visit the Westover Migrant Labor Camp but had been told that our chances of getting in were not good because the camp owners, the Somerset Growers Association, were not interested in visits from writers and photographers. The camp, for many years a migrant barracks, had been used during World War II to house German prisoners. Three years ago, Maryland health inspectors had declared the camp unfit for human habitation and recommended that it be closed. But it was still open, and over five hundred migrant workers were living there this harvest season.

As it turned out, there wasn't the slightest chance that we could have got into the camp that day. Early that morning, about three hours before we arrived, officers from the Immigration and Naturalization Service swooped into the camp on a surprise raid, looking for illegal aliens. In the ensuing panic, many migrant workers had run into some nearby woods to hide, but the officers still had arrested seventeen Mexicans and one Salvadoran and charged them with being in the country illegally. It was not a day for outsiders with notebook and camera to visit the camp.

Instead, we went looking for the Migrant Head Start day-care center and found it in a beautifully equipped and air-conditioned elementary school in the little town of Marion. Dianne Brooks, the friendly, energetic center director, is a teacher at nearby Princess Anne Elementary School during the school year. She showed

Fortino and Ramona Garcia, migrant farmworkers, in their trailer home at 6Ls Farm near Naples, Florida. Fortino works as a truck driver during tomato harvests on 6Ls farms in Florida, South Carolina, Maryland, and Pennsylvania, providing him with year-round employment.

Ramona working as a migrant aid in the Head Start Child-Care Center in Marion, Maryland.

us around the center, and we saw the children—107 in all, and most from the Westover camp—watching *Sesame Street* on television, finger painting, and playing with blocks and peg games. Babies slept in their pink and blue cribs.

I thought about these same children sitting all day, day after day, in the hot, condemned former prisoner-of-war barracks that is the Westover Migrant Labor Camp. That is where they would have been if it were not for the Migrant Head Start Program. I couldn't think of a better way to spend some government tax money.

5
Single Migrants
in the Streams

Albert Lee, Immokalee, Florida, a former migrant, now a paralegal on the staff of Florida Rural Legal Services, which helps migrants. "I was brought to Florida from Louisiana twenty years ago in a tramp bus and sold for $10," he says. The farmer paid the bus driver $10 for each of the forty-three workers he delivered.

S INGLE MIGRANTS—those who travel alone—make up the majority of migrant farmworkers in America. They are mostly young men, although some older ones drift in the migrant streams year after year. Many crew leaders pick single men for their crews because they are easier to transport and house in labor camps. Migrants who travel alone may be married but leave their families behind when they join a crew and go "on the season."

The worst stereotypes of migrants originate in single men who follow the crops. In the minds of many people, they are winos, skid-row bums, and other derelicts recruited by "day haulers" who supply workers to farmers on a daily basis. It is true that such men can be found in the fields and labor camps in every agricultural state, but it is also true that they make up only a tiny percentage of the total of migrant workers. Unfortunately, they are the ones who have been most publicized and who stay in the public mind.

Many single migrants are young Hispanics, blacks, and occasionally whites who are continuing the life they knew as children with migrant parents. It is a familiar life and the only way they know to make a living. The home bases for most of them are Texas, Florida, and California. But increasingly, the ten thousand migrant labor camps of America are being filled with men from outside the country. They are here without families, and they have come to find a job, to work, and—in many cases, perhaps most—to send money home to wives, children, parents, brothers, and sisters who are mired in hopeless poverty.

Illegal Aliens

The most serious immigration problem facing the United States to day is illegal entry. Estimates of illegal aliens now living in the United States range from three to six million, over 90 percent of them from Mexico. Hundreds of thousands are caught by the Immigration and Naturalization Service border patrols every year and are returned to Mexico or the other countries from which they come, but new thousands cross the Rio Grande looking for work in the United States every day.

Of the millions of aliens illegally in the United States, an estimated six hundred thousand work part time or full time as migrant farm laborers. This number is three times the estimated total of adult U.S. citizens and legal residents working as agricultural migrants. According to an article in the *New York Times,* California's agricultural labor force of about three hundred thousand workers in 1984 was made up mostly of illegal aliens from Mexico.

The problems caused legal migrant farmworkers by illegal aliens can hardly be overstated. Desperate for work and in constant fear of being caught and deported, illegal aliens will take almost any wages offered and live in isolated, unlicensed labor camps under the most wretched conditions, camps that Wendell Rollason, executive director of the Redlands Christian Migrant Association, has called "hell holes."

Most illegal aliens enter the United States by crossing the border into Texas, New Mexico, Arizona, and California, and large numbers of them stay in those states. Their presence adds enormously to an oversupply of farm labor that already exists in the West and Southwest. Since the illegal aliens will work for less, thousands of farmworkers who are citizens and legal residents must migrate to other states to find jobs.

High concentrations of illegal aliens cause communities severe problems of health, housing, education, and unemployment. For vegetable and fruit growers and food processing companies, however, these illegal job-seekers provide an abundant harvest labor force that is most welcome since it makes recruiting easy and keeps labor costs down.

The worst cases of peonage in America always involve illegal aliens. The Farmworker Justice Fund is a private organization that gives legal aid to agricultural workers; its annual report for 1983 states: "During the past few years a significant number of farmworkers have been brought into the state [of Arkansas] to harvest tomatoes. Many of these workers are undocumented aliens who have been smuggled into the United States by crew leaders and virtually sold to Arkansas growers. They have been kept in inaccessible labor camps under the most deplorable conditions and required to work for next to nothing."

The Migrant Legal Action Program is also a private organization, but it is supported entirely by U.S. government funds. During congressional testimony in 1982, this organization, together with others testifying, reported a case of illegal aliens from Mexico being delivered to an East Coast grower for five hundred dollars each. The workers were to receive no wages until they had worked off the "purchase" price. Since they were charged for their food and almost all other expenses, it would have been practically impossible for them to ever have worked their way out of debt. In this case, a court action freed the workers and awarded them five hundred dollars each, but there was no further punishment for the grower or the crew leader.

These cases illustrate the helplessness of illegal aliens. They rarely know how to seek legal aid and in any case are afraid to protest for fear of being deported. The Farmworkers Justice Fund estimates that as many as a hundred thousand farmworkers in America may be held in conditions of peonage.

It is not against the law in the United States to hire illegal aliens. The proposed Simpson-Mazzoli Immigration Act would change that and make employers responsible for assuring that everyone they hire is a U.S. citizen or, if an alien, has approval from the government to work in the United States. Employers who hire illegal aliens could be fined or, with repeated violations, put in jail. Despite intense efforts by the bill's supporters in both Democratic and Republican parties, it failed to pass the House of Representatives in 1983 and 1984.

Great pressure was brought against the bill by agricultural and other business interests that benefit from the large pool of cheap labor provided by illegal aliens. These interests argue that it is unfair to make employers agents of government in determining whether people have a legal right to work. It should be noted that many Hispanic leaders in the United States also oppose the bill because they are afraid it would be used to discriminate against Hispanics. Overly cautious employers, they say, might refuse to hire anyone who looks as if he or she is of Mexican or other Hispanic background.

The problem is a very difficult one that may never be resolved by a change in the immigration law. One thing is certain, however. As long as illegal aliens flood the labor market, U.S. farmworkers will suffer from unemployment and low wages.

Benito Lopez, a former migrant and founder of United Migrant Association in Florida. The Association, which publicizes migrants' problems and helps in legal disputes, has 6,500 members.

The Haitians

The nearby Caribbean country of Haiti is one of the poorest in the world. Eighty-five percent of the country's population of six million lives below the World Bank's absolute poverty level figure of $135 per year. One child out of every five dies before the age of four. Haiti's food production is declining by 2.5 percent every year. And according to a House of Representatives Foreign Affairs Committee staff report, "Haitian government corruption and insensitivity to the plight of the average Haitian are pervasive."

Haitians have been coming to the United States for a long time, both legally and illegally, in relatively small numbers, but in 1980 and 1981 they began to arrive by the tens of thousands. They did not try to go through immigration procedures, for they knew that that would take years, or, more likely, that they would never be allowed to come.

So they came by small boats, traveling the Windward Passage between Cuba and Haiti. Hundreds were drowned when their leaky old boats capsized in the rough seas, but thousands of Haitians reached the coast of south Florida alive. Many were captured by immigration agents and put in detention camps, but large numbers eluded the border patrols and disappeared into the Florida countryside.

Most of these Haitian illegal aliens—over 90 percent single men—became farmworkers, first in Florida, later filtering into the migrant stream up the Eastern Seaboard. The labor camps and small rural towns where they found shelter offered some isolation from immigration officers, and the work in the fields and orchards provided quick cash, which they desperately needed.

In 1982 I talked to a Haitian named Raymond, who had been in Florida for almost a year; he was working as a day laborer on a vegetable farm near Delray Beach and earning about twenty-five dollars a day. Many of the Haitians I talked to at that time were young, unmarried men who had come to the United States because they had lost hope of finding jobs in their country; but some, like Raymond, had risked their lives out of desperate need to save their starving families.

Raymond, who was forty years old, had left his wife and twelve children in Haiti. "We have a small piece of land in Haiti," he told me, "but the soil is poor, there is no money for fertilizer, and every year there seems less food for the table. Sometimes I worked in banana plantations and on road repair, but the money I earned was very little. Three of our children died or there would have been fifteen. When the last one died—she was but two years old—I said to my wife, 'I must go to America.'

"So I borrowed passage money from the moneylender. I said, 'I will send money to pay you back.' He smiled and said, 'I am not worried.' What he meant was that if I did not pay back the loan and the interest, he would take my land, and then my wife and children would truly starve.

"And so I am here in Florida, and I am sending money back, and my wife has written me that our children are healthier than they have ever been. I pray every day that an immigration officer will not come and take me to a detention center. I have no green card, no permit to work. But I must work or my children will die."

I never saw Raymond again. I don't know whether he continued to be successful in avoiding immigration authorities. But thousands of Haitians have avoided them or are fighting deportation by claiming to be political refugees. By federal court order, they can no longer be kept in detention while they are waiting for their cases to be heard—hearings which may take years to schedule.

Most Haitian illegals begin their survival in the United States by working in the fields and orchards of Florida and other East Coast states. Many study English in special night classes for migrants and leave the migrant stream as quickly as they can find other jobs. But they still add to the already serious oversupply of

Haitian migrants attend a night school operated for them in Marion, Maryland.

farm labor. Although the great Haitian flood of the early 1980s has pinched off, new arrivals still land on the shores of south Florida.

Legal Entry: Jamaicans and Others

A lively reggae song blared from the cassette player in the corner. Bright travel posters picturing Jamaica vacation paradises decorated the walls, and pungent smells of coconut turnovers and curried goat meat filled the room. The tiny eight-room cafe in the West Indian section of Washington, D.C., seemed an odd place to be talking about cutting sugarcane in Florida, but that was what I was doing.

Jeremiah is a taxi driver, one of many Jamaicans following that trade in the nation's capital. I had been introduced to him by my friend Jean-Keith Fagan, a Washington editor and writer who also happens to be a Jamaican. Jeremiah and I were the cafe's only customers and not very good ones, with nothing but cups of coffee in front of us.

"Why you want to talk about Jamaicans cutting cane in Florida?" he asked me, his Jamaican accent delightful. "You go to Belle Glade down there. You see plenty."

I thought about the great overhang of smoke in the sky, the red glow at dusk, the smell of burning leaves from the sugarcane fields being prepared for harvest near Belle Glade.

"I've been there," I said. "I've seen lots of Jamaicans packed in trucks riding to the fields. But the cane growers don't exactly have the welcome mat out for writers."

Jeremiah laughed. "You right," he said. "I cut cane five years in Florida and I never see anyone much but Jamaicans. Except people in stores where I buy things before I go back to Jamaica."

I was talking to Jeremiah because he was one of tens of thousands of strong, young Jamaican men who have been brought to Florida for the past three decades or more by sugar companies and growers to cut cane. Section H-2 of the Immigration and Nationality Act of 1952 authorizes importing temporary foreign workers into the United States if no domestic workers can be found to do the jobs. The sugarcane growers have been successful in convincing the secretary of labor that Americans cannot cut sugarcane or do not want to.

"I've heard that lots of Jamaicans want to come to the United States to cut cane," I said to Jeremiah.

"Are you kidding?" he said. "They crazy to come. They do anything to come."

"I've heard working conditions are dangerous," I said, "that one-third of all Jamaican cane cutters working in Florida suffer some kind of injury."

Jeremiah shrugged. "Everything dangerous," he said. "I been robbed twice driving a cab in Washington."

I would have liked to ask Jeremiah how he happened to be driving a taxi in Washington, but I didn't want to change the subject.

"Tell me why Jamaicans want to cut cane in Florida," I said, "and how you get selected to come."

Jeremiah drank some of his coffee. "Almost everybody poor in Jamaica," he said, "especially in rural parts. If you know how to cut cane, you poor. You bet on that. If they pick you to cut cane in United States, you get rich. Maybe you save three thousand dollars in a year if you try. They send part of your pay to Jamaica and hold it for you there so you won't spend it all buying things before you come home.

"When the cane cutters come home in chartered airplane, they loaded with TV sets, radios, watches, gold rings. They dressed in jeans, plaid shirts, heavy boots. They best dressed in village. Married men send all their money home, and they buy house, even a farm if they cut cane a few years. Lots of married men picked to go to Florida because they work hard to send money home."

"And how are men picked?" I asked again.

"Politics to start," Jeremiah said. "Politicians all over Jamaica get to pick a few men in their district. Then the men get called to Kingston. No politics there. They pick the best, the strongest. They look at your hands to see if you a real cane cutter. Men from sugar companies in Florida help do the picking. Maybe half or more don't get picked and have to go back to village."

"Do you think Americans could cut cane?" I asked.

"Jamaicans better," Jeremiah said.

"But could Americans learn to be good cutters?"

"If they strong," Jeremiah said. "But Jamaicans need jobs."

I took a piece of paper from my pocket. "I want to read you a statement by Florida Legal Services lawyers to one of our congressional subcommittees," I said. " ' The Jamaican H-2 worker is for the cane growers the perfect farm laborer—a man of the barracks, a man in a camp who spends all of his time under supervision if not under surveillance, surrounded by barbed wire. A man without a family who will never be part of the larger community; who has no hope of a better job or indeed any job in this country other than swinging a machete eight hours a day. A man who will never vote in Florida, never join a union, and never go to court to correct an injustice.'

"What do you think of that?" I asked Jeremiah.

He had listened very carefully. He was silent a moment and then he chuckled. "Yeah," he said. "That good. Sound like my poly sci book at G.W.U. That good writing. But Jamaica man still crazy to come to Florida and cut cane. All how you look at it, I guess."

The irony is that Section H-2 was originally written into the Immigration and Nationality Act of 1952 to protect American workers from a flood of foreign competition. The law states that foreign workers may be brought into the United States on a temporary basis only if the attorney general certifies that qualified American workers are not available. The attorney general has delegated the approval responsibility to the secretary of labor. The clear purpose of H-2 is to make certain that Americans have first opportunity in the job market.

H-2 is a classic "America first" statute that has provided protection for all of the country's workers, skilled and unskilled, except those in agriculture. In the case of farmworkers, the law has been turned around and used as a legal means of bringing thousands of men from Jamaica, the Dominican Republic, and Mexico every year to harvest cane in Florida, apples in Virginia, onions in Texas, grapefruit in Arizona, and other crops in other states.

Labor unions, the Farmworkers Justice Fund, and Migrant

A Jamaican migrant cuts cane in central Florida.

Legal Aid have fought bitterly against the way the Department of Labor regularly approves agricultural companies' and growers' requests for foreign workers under H-2. These organizations argue that imported foreign laborers take away tens of thousands of jobs from unemployed or underemployed American farm-workers who are competent to do the work or, in the case of cutting sugarcane, who could easily be trained to do it. Evidence is overwhelming that they are right.

Why then do the agricultural companies and growers prefer foreign to American workers? The answer is not that foreign workers are cheaper, because the H-2 law stipulates that imported labor must be paid at least as much as domestic workers would receive in order not to depress wages. It is true that growers do not have to pay Social Security tax or, in most cases, unemployment insurance on the wages of H-2 workers. But they do have to pay transportation costs to bring the workers to the United States and return them.

The answer seems to lie in the absolute control that growers have over H-2 foreign workers, particularly in the case of the sugarcane companies and growers. They help select the workers. They decide where they will be housed. Since the foreign workers do not have cars, they can easily control their movements. The sugar companies set production quotas; if a worker does not meet his quota, he can be sent back to Jamaica without any right of appeal. Only 60 percent of the H-2 labor force is retained from one year to the next. The fear of being sent back before his contract is completed, or of not being selected for another year, ensures that almost every worker will exhaust himself at his labor.

The H-2 system works very well for the agricultural companies that use (or abuse) it, and there is no question that it has been a great boon to thousands of Jamaicans and other foreign workers. But under the law, the responsibility of the U.S. government is to see that American workers are not deprived of jobs unfairly by foreign competition. For many years now the H-2 law has been used to do just the opposite of what it is intended to do. It has been taking work away from Americans.

Perhaps Jeremiah said it best: "All how you look at it." Clearly, the agricultural companies, growers' associations, and the U.S. government have not been looking at it through the eyes of American farmworkers.

6
A Season in Apples

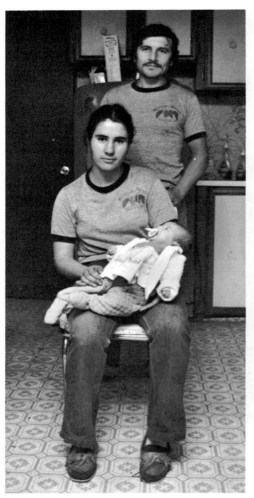

Migrant couples in upper New York State.

E VERY SPRING, migrant farmworkers leave their home bases in Texas and Florida and arrive in thousands of agricultural communities across the United States. They stay a few weeks or a few months: just the amount of time it takes to harvest the potatoes, lettuce, peaches, or whatever crops are the economic heart of a particular place. Then they leave.

The system is perfect for these "receiving" or "up-stream" communities. They must have a large number of workers at harvest time, but the financial strain of housing and feeding the workers all year just to have them available for the short time they are needed would be impossible. There is no problem, however. The migrant workers will be on their way the day the harvest is finished. They will not linger.

Wayne County, New York, receives about four thousand migrants every summer and fall. It is beautiful country, that part of western New York that touches the south shore of Lake On-

tario and rolls gently southward to the Finger Lakes. Though the
cities of Rochester and Syracuse are close by, this is farmland,
superb farmland with rich black muck soil that yields finest-
quality vegetables. Wayne County, together with the surround-
ing area, is the fourth-largest onion producer in America, and the
seventh-largest lettuce producer. Potatoes are an important
money crop.

But October belongs to apples. Although potatoes and carrots
are still being harvested, for the next two months the apple is
king. Rows of trees burdened with Delicious, Rhode Island
Greenings, and Romes stretch out across the low hills until they
become a blur on the horizon. Some of the small trees are so
heavily laden with fruit that they are bent almost to the ground.

"Will they break?" I asked an orchard owner, when Paul and
I visited Wayne County in early October.

He laughed and said, "Never saw one break. They'll stand up
straight as soon as they're picked."

The pickers begin to arrive in force from Florida the last week
in September. Crew leaders bring their gangs of single men in old
school buses; families, both black and Hispanic, come in cars,
station wagons, and panel trucks crammed with people and
household goods. Most of them have been here before and know
exactly where they are going. They head straight for places like
Three Mile Camp, Van Dusen Camp, and houses where workers
for the big Senco Farms' orchards stay.

The 170 migrant camps that dot Wayne County are all
packed. Most of the camps are small, just shanties with outhouses
and common showers. Some have a building for cooking and
eating. There are a few big houses with eight or more rooms, some
barracks, and some trailers. It is a motley collection of housing
but as good as the migrants are likely to find in other places they
will work during the year.

"They're just going to be here a few weeks," one grower said
to me.

And that, I am sure, is just what the grower in the migrants' next stop will say.

On a cool, sunny afternoon, we went to a MacIntosh orchard. The sharp, clean, sweet smell of apples filled the air. I pulled one from a tree and ate it; it was cool and crisp, and the taste was sharp, clean, and sweet. I remembered reading that in ancient times apples were considered to be the fruit of the gods, and at this moment I could understand why. I could also understand why a lot of romantic nonsense has been spoken and written about migrants working in a clean, healthful outdoors environment.

Near where I stood, a Hispanic family of four, mother and father and two teenage daughters, worked intently. They had arrived from Florida that morning and had lost no time getting to the orchard. They attacked the trees as a team, two working on long ladders at the top, two picking at ground level. Big red and green plastic bags hung from their shoulders, and they filled them with astonishing speed. No motion was wasted. One hand would plunge into the leaves, and in the same instant the other would come out of the branches grasping two or three apples. Yet even at that speed, they managed a gentle twist so that the stem would come off with the apple.

The family could strip an average tree of its fruit in about twenty minutes. They emptied their bags into big, twenty-bushel wooden bins, being careful not to bruise the apples. These apples were going to the fresh market, so the family would be paid twelve dollars for each bin filled. Apples to be processed into applesauce or apple butter at the big Duffy Mott plant nearby would bring them only eight dollars a bin. Processing apples can be picked much faster, even shaken from the trees.

A good worker can make $250 or even $300 a week picking apples. This family probably would average a thousand a week for the six or eight weeks of the harvest. Probably they would

This Hispanic woman fills her apple bucket in an orchard in New York State.

save most of it, and they would need it. The citrus harvest to which they would be returning was certain to be meager because of two years' freezes. The apple bonanza would help them survive the winter months in their home base.

Another day, Clifford DeMay, manager of Senco Farms, took us around to several parts of the big corporate apple orchard that sprawls over 2,750 acres in Wayne County. Senco Farms is owned by Seneca Foods, which in turn is a part of the S. S. Pierce Corporation. That is the arrangement more and more today in American agriculture. It is called agribusiness. The migrant laborer picking apples in the great orchard does not think of himself as part of a corporate structure, but he is: a microscopic part, to be sure, but a vital one—perhaps like a rivet in the wing of an American Airlines corporate airplane.

One part of the orchard we visited was being picked by a crew from Florida. They were all black, all men, mostly young. And they were good. They worked intently, silently, filling the big wooden bins that were weathered gray from years in the orchard. The crew leader, a tall older man with a lean, weatherbeaten face, walked around quietly encouraging his men. He told me that he had been coming to the apple harvest in Wayne County for the past thirty years.

"Used to pick with the daddies of some of these fellas," he said.

"You have a good crew," I said.

He nodded. "They like you, they work hard."

I rode with DeMay—Cliff as everyone calls him—to another location. It was hard to talk because his two-way car radio kept breaking in with problems for him to solve. Workers hadn't shown up in one part of the orchard. There was an accident someplace else. They were having trouble setting up a meeting he wanted with his crew leaders that night. In each case Cliff told the voice at the other end what to do.

"Too much fruit is being bruised," he told me. "I've got to have a session with my crew leaders about that."

At the next stop I asked Cliff if I could climb a ladder and pick some apples. "It's against company policy for a visitor to break a leg," he said, "but go ahead."

He found a bag for me, and I tried to pick up one of the long aluminum ladders lying on the ground. I staggered with it and almost fell before a young worker came running over and helped me ease it into a tree. I climbed about halfway up the ladder and started picking. On my first try the apple came off without the stem. That was no good, I knew; the hole could cause the apple to spoil.

I found that I was holding on to the ladder with one hand and picking with the other. I knew that wasn't right, but when I let loose, I wobbled. Finally, I discovered that by leaning into the ladder and putting my weight against the rungs, I could pick with both hands. I was aware that my hands were not exactly working together like parts of a machine, but I thought I was doing well and, when I climbed down after a few minutes, felt rather good about my performance.

The young worker who had helped me with the ladder came over. I had seen him go up and down his ladder with a full bag twice while I was picking. He looked in my bag; it was a little less than half full.

He grinned and said, "You pick like that, you starve."

On the way back to Cliff's office we stopped at one of the Senco crew quarters, a big two-story house on the edge of the orchard. Small individual rooms would hold two or more men, but it was the middle of the afternoon and no one was there. I walked through the kitchen and big common room that contained a couple of tables and some chairs. The place was undecorated, curtainless but clean enough. I was astonished to see a Wurlitzer juke box in one corner.

"They like music," Cliff said, and he added, "you should see

A Haitian migrant picks apples in New York State, Wayne County.

this place on Friday night, after payday. Whiskey, wine, gambling. Sometimes gamblers come from the city and clean out the whole house, five or six thousand dollars."

"Do you do anything?" I asked.

"Sure. I talk to them," Cliff said, "but what else can you do? It's their money. Some of them blow their pay in one night, money they've worked all week for. You and I spend our money on cars and houses. They've got their own ideas. They've got their own values. They make money and spend it having a good time."

I did not doubt that he was right. I was sure that there are thousands of young single migrants who spend their money on their idea of a good time. They know they will never have enough money for a house or perhaps even a car, or maybe they just don't think about it. But I had met many others in the stream of single migrants who were sending home almost everything they made. They had their own values, too.

I had thought the house was empty, but just before we left I passed a room with the door partly open and saw a man lying in bed. He had a cover over him, but he was not asleep. I asked him if he was sick.

He nodded. "Sick. Got the flu and I can't pick a lick."

Can't pick a lick. It was a bit of migrant jargon I had heard before, and it was the worst thing that could happen in the migrant world: to have work and not be able to do it. For them, there is no sick leave with pay. For them, the rule is simple: no work, no pay.

"I'll be pickin' tomorrow," he said.

Basil Dobush is director of the Wayne County Tutorial Program for migrant children in grades kindergarten through twelve. Over 450 migrant children were receiving tutoring help in the school program in the fall of 1984, and Basil's staff of thirty-three tutors was also working with a number of dropouts who had hopes or intentions of getting back into school at some future time. The program is paid for by special U.S. government funds set aside for migrant education. Any county in the United States where migrants work can apply for these funds. Many do, but unfortunately many others do not.

Basil has been with the Wayne County Tutorial Program for years. The program concentrates on help with such basic skills as reading, writing, and mathematics, but tutoring in specific courses—history, social studies, literature—is undertaken when necessary.

Basil is reasonably optimistic. "Migrant students carry a lot of problems with them," he told us. "Different schools, teachers, books, courses. Some of them miss part of the school year. Some

Kathy Fox, director of a Cornell University literacy program for migrants in Wayne County. The migrants are taught in night classes by community volunteer tutors.

have language problems—not much English. Hardly any have the right conditions to study at home. But over the years they're doing better. We have a 50 percent continuity rate—students coming back year after year—so I'm not just guessing about that. And more are graduating from high school."

On the subject of prejudice, Basil was not so optimistic. "Some local parents don't want their children to go to school with migrant children," he said. "Enrollment has actually dropped in some schools with large migrant enrollments. We used to put migrants in separate classes, but that's a thing of the past."

At North Rose–Wolcott High School in Wayne County, I talked with some migrant students; all were receiving tutorial help of some kind. I first met Thomas Jessie, a seventeen-year-old junior from Haines City, Florida, who lives and travels with his father, T. J. Jessie, just the two of them. Thomas's father picks oranges around Haines City and in other places in Florida from December until the season ends in the spring. Thomas picks along with his father on weekends and during school breaks. He doesn't miss school if he can help it.

In the summer they come to New York to work in the onion fields and, in October and November, to pick apples. It becomes weekend work again for Thomas as soon as school begins in New York. This has been the pattern of his life ever since he can remember, just his father and he dividing their lives between Florida and New York, picking oranges and apples, and, for Thomas, going to school.

"My daddy taught me to work," Thomas said with a touch of pride.

One year T. J. Jessie decided they should stay in one place so that Thomas's schooling would not be interrupted. He was able to get a job in a factory in Niagara Falls, New York, but the winter was terrible.

"One day the snow was so deep my daddy couldn't find his car," Thomas said with a smile. "We went back to Florida, and he started picking oranges again."

"What are you going to do after you finish high school?" I asked.

"I'd like to learn to operate heavy equipment," he said. "If I can't do that, I want to join the Marines."

"But you won't stay in migrant farm work?" I asked.

Thomas considered his answer. "It's been all right for my daddy and me," he said. "I haven't minded it. But I'm not gonna do it after I get out of high school."

Thomas's quietly thoughtful answer was convincing, and I had the feeling he would carry out his plans for the future. But I knew that many young migrant men and women stay in the migrant life or go back to it, even after they have prevailed over great odds and finished high school.

"It is just too easy for them to drift back to the fields and orchards," Estela Rodriguez once said to me. "They get a high school diploma, but they don't use it as a stepping-stone to something else, as least too many of them don't. Some of them think they can't do anything else just because they are migrants. Others have trouble getting a job or getting into college, and they give up too soon. They know they can make money picking. They've done it since they were children. So they come back."

Estela thinks there should be a special program for young migrant men and women who have finished high school, one that would give them special skills and job training. She has tried to get such a program started but so far without success.

The problem of what migrant youth do after high school was on my mind when I talked with Bernard Goodwin, another migrant student at North Rose–Wolcott High School. Bernard is seventeen, a senior, and also from Florida, the town of Winter Haven, where his parents work in the citrus groves.

"Winter Haven," I said. "The Boston Red Sox do their spring training there. You ever see them?"

Bernard nodded. "I sell popcorn at some of their games," he said.

But basketball, he told me, was his game. That was no surprise. I judged him to be six feet two or three, and he moved with the easy grace that comes so naturally to good basketball players.

"Guard?" I asked.

"Small forward," he said.

Bernard is on the varsity of Winter Haven High School. His family—mother, father, two brothers, two sisters—come to New York every year for the apple harvest, arriving about mid-September and getting back to Winter Haven in time for Bernard to play basketball. He hopes to get a basketball scholarship to the University of South Florida in Tampa. He said that the tutoring program in math and English was helping him and that he was working hard because good grades would help his scholarship chances.

Bernard Goodwin, a migrant and student at North Rose-Wolcott High School in New York State.

"Do you spend much time picking oranges and apples?" I asked.

"My folks have never made me pick," he said. "But I do it when I want something—clothes, or records or spending money. Same with my brothers and sisters."

Once again I thought of how tempting and natural it must be for the children of migrants, born to the system and knowing it well, to turn back to the harvests whenever there is disappointment or financial stress in the nonmigrant world.

"It's rather like money growing on trees, isn't it?" I said.

"Yes," Bernard said, "like that."

But the money tree is a lifelong trap, and I hoped that Bernard would play basketball in college.

I talked to other migrant students at North Rose–Wolcott: Carla Miller, a tall, willowy girl who hopes someday to be a model, and Jannette and Kelvin Rivers, an attractive brother and sister who come to New York every year with their parents and other brothers and sisters. They leave their home in Union

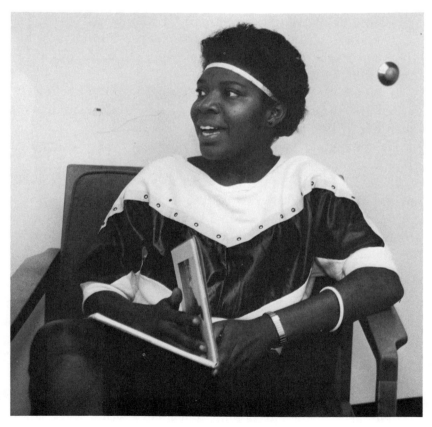

Jannette Rivers

Springs, Alabama, arriving in time for the cherry harvest and returning to Alabama after the apples are harvested. Jannette and Kelvin work in the orchards during the summer but not after school starts. Both see college in their future; Jannette told me with pride that their older sister was salutatorian of her high school class in Union Springs last year and that she was now in college on a scholarship.

I asked Kelvin, a sophomore, if he had any notion yet of what he might study in college.

"I'm interested in art and computer science," he said.

"Those fields are rather far apart," I commented.

"I know," he said, "but I've got plenty of time to decide which one to concentrate on. And maybe I can figure out a way to make them come together."

Kelvin was so sharp and articulate that I couldn't believe he needed the tutoring help available to the migrant students. I asked him if he felt he needed it.

He smiled and said, "It's there. Why not take advantage of it?"

I asked Kelvin if he thought there was any prejudice toward migrant students on the part of local students.

"I don't think so," he said. "I haven't felt any, and it's not a problem with migrant kids I know. But it's hard to develop relationships when you're just here for two months every year."

"What do you think is the biggest problems for migrant students?" I asked.

Kelvin considered his answer only a moment. "Frustration," he said. "You get something started, you have a teacher you like, and a few weeks later, you're gone."

The migrant students I talked to seemed so special that I asked the teacher in charge of the tutoring program if only the best had been selected for me to talk with.

"Not at all," she said. "I told all of them a writer was coming who wanted to talk to migrant students and asked if anyone was

Zona Wycoff, a "settled out" migrant in New York State.

interested. You met the curious ones. The ones who said yes."

I should have felt good when I left the school, and I did. But I didn't kid myself. I knew the young men and women I had talked with *were* special. They were the ones who had persisted and were getting their education. I knew that for every Thomas Jessie and Jannette Rivers, there were ten teenage migrants who had quit school and were working in the orchards and fields wherever crops were being harvested in the country.

By the time the last apples are picked, the days are increasingly cool, the nights are growing cold, and most migrants are on their way south. But a few stay. They "settle out" of the stream and make New York their home. Migrants always talk about settling out in the places where they work the harvest seasons, but only the most determined do so. The decision to face the cold winters around Lake Ontario is especially hard for people who have lived most of their lives in Florida and south Texas.

But the schools are good, jobs are available for some in the Seneca or Duffy Mott food processing plants, and family members can work the vegetable and fruit harvests in summer and fall without moving. Most of the towns of Wayne County have communities of ex-migrants who live in poor, small houses. Just as in their migrant days, they stay close together, even organize their own small churches in some cases.

One woman, born and raised in Florida but now a New Yorker, said to me, "We don't go on the season anymore, but we're still migrants to most people. To ourselves, too, I guess."

And yet it is a step, a big step, for people who have spent their lives following the crops.

7
The Long Season

A Guatemalan Indian child.

E VERY YEAR in November and December they return: the
shabby, discarded school buses, the trucks, station wagons,
and old gas-guzzlers with huge trunks. They are filled with
men, women, and children who have spent the summer and early
fall harvesting crops in North Carolina, Maryland, New York,
Indiana, Ohio, Illinois, Michigan, Wisconsin, and other states in
the East and Midwest. Now they converge on Florida for the long
season of winter and spring citrus and vegetable production. For
the next six or seven months this single state must somehow try
to provide work, housing, and health care for a labor force that
had been spread over a third of the nation.

No one knows how many migrants return to Florida at year's
end or come for the first time; the best informed guesses range
from seventy-five thousand to twice that. Some come back to
groves and fields where they have worked for years, and they will
have jobs unless there is weather disaster or crop disease. Others

only hope they will be among the lucky ones who arrive in the right place at the right time.

Overload

South Florida is famous for its winter vegetables and its splendid winter weather. The same sun that warms the golden beaches of Palm Beach County and Miami's Dade County for basking tourists ripens the tomatoes, snap beans, squash, and cucumbers of the great farms farther inland. Over forty thousand migrants will crowd the squalid labor camps of Palm Beach County alone. Thousands of others, those who have jobs and those who do not, will squeeze into towns in the agricultural areas, hoping to find a house to share, a room to rent, or a doorway to sleep in.

These towns cannot cope with the human flood that descends on them. Some, like Belle Glade near the southern end of Lake Okeechobee, have almost stopped trying. Nearly forty years ago, in her history of the Everglades, *River of Grass,* Marjory Stoneman Douglas called Belle Glade an "Everglades slum" and a "human jungle." This town of seventeen thousand people is probably much worse today than it was at the time she wrote about it. A survey five years ago found half of the town's six thousand dwellings to be substandard and 16 percent of them unfit for human habitation. An estimated eight thousand Haitians, hoping for work in the sugarcane and vegetable fields, have crowded into Belle Glade.

An article about Belle Glade by *Miami Herald* staff writer Randy Loftis in the October 28, 1984, issue of the paper contained these paragraphs:

In the isolated western reaches of Florida's richest county [Palm Beach], thousands of men, women, and children awaken each day in bad-dream barracks of cement-block rooms, 10 feet square, in rooming houses with frayed electri-

cal wires and floors of sagging plywood or dusty, bare concrete, in trailers giving up the struggle to stay intact. . . .

The city's low-income rental business is lucrative, at
least on paper. Most tenants of one-room units with no
plumbing, heat or air conditioning pay $35 to $55 a week.
Trailer tenants pay as much as $500 a month—amounts that
rival rents for three- to six-room apartments on the urban
coast. A typical 25-unit building can produce almost $50,000
a year in gross income.

Larger towns like Belle Glade and Immokalee farther to the
west on the edge of Big Cypress Swamp may receive some attention from the press and state agencies. Small towns are simply
overlooked. Such a place is Indiantown, a community of about
thirty-five hundred permanent residents two hours' drive from
Miami. To get there, Paul and I drove up Highway 95 past some
of the most glittering names on the Florida map: Bal Harbour,
Fort Lauderdale, Pompano Beach, Boca Raton, Delray Beach,
Palm Beach. At Riviera Beach we took State Highway 710 to
Indiantown, which is located a few miles from Lake Okeechobee
on St. Lucie Canal, a part of Florida's Intercoastal Waterway.

The land around Indiantown is excellent not only for all kinds
of winter vegetables but also for citrus crops. The isolation of the
little town makes it attractive to illegal aliens from Mexico and
Central America and to Haitians, who like to keep within com-
municating distance of the Little Haiti section of Miami. The
backroads around Indiantown are dotted with small, nondescript
migrant camps, rundown houses and barracks holding twenty to
thirty single men or half a dozen families.

Indiantown itself has some sections with nice houses and
some, like an area called Booker Park, with tiny cinder-block
houses where two or three migrant families crowd into a single
unit. A small four-room house in Booker Park rents for four
hundred dollars a month, and the tenants pay the electricity bill.

In another part of town, one large concrete building, which is divided into many one- and two-room units, is known to everyone as the Roach Palace.

The purpose of our visit to Indiantown was to talk with Father Frank O'Loughlin, a parish priest at the local Holy Cross Catholic Church. His name had come up repeatedly in our travels as one who knows all there is to know about the plight of migrants in Florida and who tries to do something about it. I had read his blistering articles on H-2 and other migrant injustices in the *Miami Herald* and *Perspectives,* a magazine devoted to civil rights.

The first person we met at Holy Cross Church, however, was Sister Carol Putnam, of whom I also had heard. I knew that five years ago Sister Carol, a Sacred Heart nun, had started Hope Rural School here in the Holy Cross Church compound, a kindergarten-through-fourth-grade school for migrant children who had been particularly deprived of a chance for regular schooling. From what I had been told, the school was a heartwarming success.

When we drove up, Sister Carol was standing beside a school bus parked near the school. After we exchanged introductions and chatted a few minutes, Sister Carol looked at the school bus and said, "Isn't it beautiful?"

It was, in fact, quite a fine-looking school bus, shiny and clean and, so far as I could tell, without a scratch on it. I said as much.

"It's a gift from Mr. Paul Newman," she said. "We got it just yesterday."

"Paul Newman, the actor?" I asked, surprised.

"Yes," Sister Carol said, and told us the story behind the gift.

The bus the school had been using to pick up migrant students from the camps around Indiantown was fourteen years old and had recently been condemned by public vehicle authorities. Sister Carol agreed that it was in hopeless condition and had to be replaced, but without a way to bring the migrant children from

Migrant children run for the school bus given to their school by Paul Newman in Indiantown, Florida.

the camps to Hope Rural School, she knew that they would soon be in the fields with their parents.

"We tried every place we could think of to get money for a new bus," Sister Carol said, "but we didn't get anyplace. We wrote to foundations all over the country. We used every contact we had and called wealthy people in the Palm Beach area. Nothing worked."

In the midst of their fruitless search, a terrible tragedy almost occurred. The old school bus with a full load of children lost its brakes at a railroad crossing and was nearly struck by an Amtrak passenger train. Only desperate floor-boarding of the gas pedal by the driver prevented a ghastly accident. It was the very next day that a $26,000 check for a new school bus arrived in the mail

Father Frank O'Loughlin with Guatemalan children, Indiantown, Florida.

from Paul Newman. It was truly money from heaven, a total surprise. The actor, who sometimes races cars on Florida tracks not far from the school, had heard of Hope Rural School's transportation crisis and had decided to help.

Sister Carol's eyes shone as she told us the story. I had always liked Paul Newman as an actor. Now I liked him as a human being.

Later, when we were sitting at a table in the churchyard with Father Frank, he referred to the gift school bus. "We need all of the outside help we can get," he said, "because Indiantown never becomes a community that can solve its own problems. There are three people for every job in this area. Families are sleeping in cars along the canal and cooking there. They'll stay there until the sheriff runs them off, but the next day they'll be back. People sleep in the citrus groves, under bridges, in doorways.

"The population of Indiantown doubles during the season, and the new ones are all poor. The town can't cope with that much poverty. There are people who want to help and they do. But the level of misery paralyzes the town."

I had not asked any question that prompted Father Frank's outpouring, but I knew that he had been showing a visiting priest around Indiantown that morning. His survey of the little town's burden of poverty and of landlords who make money out of it —a survey he doubtless had made hundreds of times—had brought his frustration to the boiling point.

"Why do they come here if there is such an oversupply of workers?" I asked.

"Where else could they go where things would be any better?" he said. "And what else can they do? There may be an extra good harvest. They may be lucky and get a few days of work a week, enough to stay alive on.

"The growers and managers of the big corporate orchards and farms welcome them. The more the better. The most recent arrivals are the most employable—the Mexicans, Salvadorans, Haitians, and now the Mayan Indians from Guatemala. They will work for whatever they can get, and they won't complain— because they can be deported. Piece rates collapse. Instead of getting seventy cents for picking a bag of oranges, they get thirty-five cents.

"American workers don't get hired because they're just not exploitable enough for the fruit and vegetable industry," Father Frank added.

For over an hour we sat in the churchyard and listened to Father Frank's bitter recital of injustices against migrants: of sugarcane companies that set up impossible qualifying tests for American men so that the Department of Labor will let the companies bring in Jamaican cutters; of immigration agents invading a church during mass to arrest undocumented Mexicans; of parents and children being separated in border patrol raids; of food stores and health clinics being used as bait for Immigration and Naturalization Service traps; of long searches to find hospitals willing to accept sick, destitute migrants from Indiantown; of giant corporations that have large agricultural holdings in the Lake Okeechobee area but refuse to accept any responsibility for what is happening there.

Two rays of brightness relieved our otherwise bleak visit to Indiantown. One was the Hope Rural School's new bus. The other was the story of the Mayan Indians from Guatemala. Caught in the middle of a vicious war between their government and guerrillas trying to overthrow it, these gentle peasants were stolen from and killed by both sides. In desperation they left Guatemala, slowly made their way through Mexico, and crossed the U.S. border, usually into Arizona. From late 1982 through the early months of 1983, over four hundred Mayan men, women, and children traveled across the United States to Indiantown.

"Why Indiantown?" I asked.

"I don't know," Sister Carol answered, "but I do know that one day I was talking with our schoolchildren about the Guatemalan Indians, and we decided to say a prayer for their safety. The next week the first truckload arrived in Indiantown. And the others have come since then."

When they arrived, the children were exhausted, malnourished, dehydrated; many were suffering from cracked, damaged feet from walking hundreds of miles through Mexico; most had skin infections and stomach and respiratory ailments. Families had no money, few clothes, and no food. No one could speak English, and for some—the old and the very young—even Spanish was limited.

In this town where misery is routine, the outpouring of sympathy and help for the Mayan Indians was immediate. Volunteers from the Holy Cross Church service center, already heavily over-

A Guatemalan Indian refugee with two children in Indiantown, Florida.

worked, found housing, clothes, and food for the desperate new arrivals. Citizens of the community not connected with Holy Cross volunteered their time to help with health problems and with teaching the Mayans the rudiments of surviving in their new home—including finding work in the fields and orchards. A local newspaper carried sympathetic articles about the ancient Mayan culture.

Today the Mayan children have recovered their health. Some are enrolled in Hope Rural School; others attend the Migrant Head Start day-care center. The problems of the Mayans continue to be severe—including a struggle with Immigration to stay in the country under refugee status—but with the help of Indiantown citizens who came together to work as a community, there is now hope in their lives.

A few months after our visit to Indiantown, I called Father Frank from my home in Virginia to ask him a question. The phone was answered by a woman with a slight Hispanic accent. "Father is not here," she said.

"Do you know when he will be back?" I asked.

"No," she said. "Father Frank had a heart attack last week. He is in a hospital in Miami." She was silent a moment and then said, "But he will be back, because we need him."

Citrus World

Central Florida is citrus country. A traveler through the rolling hills of seemingly endless orchards sometimes has the sensation of being at sea. Most of the state's fifty million citrus trees are in central Florida, as are most of the huge fruit-packing plants and the orange and grapefruit concentrate factories. This is also the land of super tourist attractions: Cypress Gardens, EPCOT Center, Circus World, Walt Disney World. But the tourist who drives to these places has no doubt about where he is. He is in Citrus World.

Haines City is in the heart of Central Florida's citrus country. Any road into this town of eleven thousand will take a visitor through orange, grapefruit, and tangerine groves. The packing plant of Orange Co., a major citrus corporation, is located there. Roadside stands along all the highways tempt travelers with bargain-price bags of fruit. The Holiday Inn outside Haines City sits practically in an orange grove.

Dorothy and Lenard Gilley live in Haines City. It seems appropriate that their small, comfortable home should be located on a street named Orange Court, because oranges have been important in their lives. Not that they were in the beginning. Dorothy and Lenard were born in rural Alabama, grew up there, and married there. They lived in the little town of Samson but worked on farms in the area. He also worked in a sawmill, she in a shirt mill.

In 1952 they moved to Florida and began a life as migrant farmworkers. They worked in the citrus groves in the winter and in the summer and fall traveled north to pick cherries, pears, strawberries, and other crops. They had two daughters who traveled with them, and the family led the true migrant life. Labor camps were their home for much of every year.

But Florida was their home base, and Haines City became their home, to which they always returned. In 1957 Lenard went to work for B. C. Cook and Sons in Haines City as the operator of a high-lift loader. This essential piece of citrus orchard equipment lifts tubs and boxes of fruit into trucks after the pickers have filled them. It was good, steady work, but the family continued to go north for picking when the citrus season ended.

A major change came in their lives in 1970 when they were able to take over payments on a high-lift loader from a friend who had to sell it. The remaining amount due on the machine was eleven thousand dollars, and it was a big financial hill to climb; but it was a chance for Lenard to go into business for himself, and they decided to try to climb that hill. Dorothy went to work in a fast-food restaurant to help.

Today they have the high-lift loader, a secondhand semi, and five trailers to go with it. They are very much in business for themselves. Lenard contracts with Orange Co. for citrus picking and hauling, and during the summer he takes his semi and two trailers to Indiana and hauls tomatoes.

The day we visited Lenard Gilley, he and his crew were picking tangerines in a grove on the outskirts of Haines City. But first Dorothy took us to Orange Co. headquarters for permission to enter the groves. We had been concerned that we might have a problem because approaching Haines City we had seen signs at the edge of every grove warning that it was illegal to enter without being decontaminated. Decontamination, we had learned, meant being sprayed with alcohol as protection against carrying citrus canker bacteria into the orchards. Citrus canker is the most

A migrant family in a citrus grove in Florida. They are part of Lenard Gilley's crew.

dreaded disease that attacks citrus trees; it is inevitably fatal to them, and there is no way to eradicate the disease except by burning infected trees.

An outbreak of the disease in 1984—the first in nearly seventy years—attacked a number of citrus nurseries, and millions of seedlings had to be destroyed. No canker had yet been found in producing groves, but everyone in the industry was terrified that it might creep in. When the canker struck, Florida was still reeling from a terrible freeze in 1983 that killed ten million trees across the state and wiped out 120,000 acres of oranges, grapefruit, and tangerines in central Florida. The seedling trees now being burned because of canker were to have been replacements for the trees lost in 1983.

Levoy Weaver at Orange Co. said we were welcome to go into the groves if we didn't mind being sprayed. It was good to have a friendly reception, and I had no doubt that Dorothy Gilley's introduction was responsible for it. One of Mr. Weaver's tasks at Orange Co. is to schedule the work of forty crews that pick in orchards around Haines City and elsewhere in the area. The freeze of 1983 greatly reduced the 1984 harvest, and Mr. Weaver's task when we saw him was to spread the available work around as fairly as possible.

"The best we can do is two or three days' work a week for the crews," he said.

I thought about the families from Florida that I had met in the apple orchards in Wayne County, New York, and I hoped they had put away a good part of the money they made in that fine harvest. They would need it during this long, meager citrus season.

Lenard Gilley met us at the edge of the tangerine grove and sprayed us with an alcohol solution from a blue plastic five-gallon container. He sprayed extra alcohol into our hands for us to rub onto our faces and necks, and he sprayed the soles of our shoes with particular care. Later that day when we visited a grapefruit orchard only a few hundred yards from the tangerines, we had to be sprayed all over again. Everyone, from picker to citrus corporation president, is grimly serious about controlling citrus canker.

"All we've got down here is trees," one migrant worker said to me. "They keep us alive half the year."

Three nights of record low temperatures in January 1985 brought what may have been the worst freeze of the century to central Florida. The citrus crop, already stunted from the cold weather of 1983, froze on the trees. In a desperate effort to save as much as possible, even office workers turned out to pick the fruit so that it could be used in making juice concentrate. For the short frantic period, migrants and their children had more work than they could do.

But it was painfully brief. In late February I called the Gilleys to get their report on conditions. "Two weeks more work and it's finished for the season," Dorothy Gilley told me. "We'll be through in early March instead of May like we usually are."

"What will the migrants do?" I asked.

"They'll start up the coast early and do anything they can until the harvests start," Dorothy said. "Some will stay around here. Food stamps will help a little."

"And Lenard and you?" I asked.

"We're in the same boat as everyone else," Dorothy said, "but no food stamps. Lenard will haul watermelons in Immokalee in May and tomatoes in Indiana this summer. With canker and freeze, no telling what the next citrus season will be like. But we'll tough it out and try again."

8
Dark Harvest

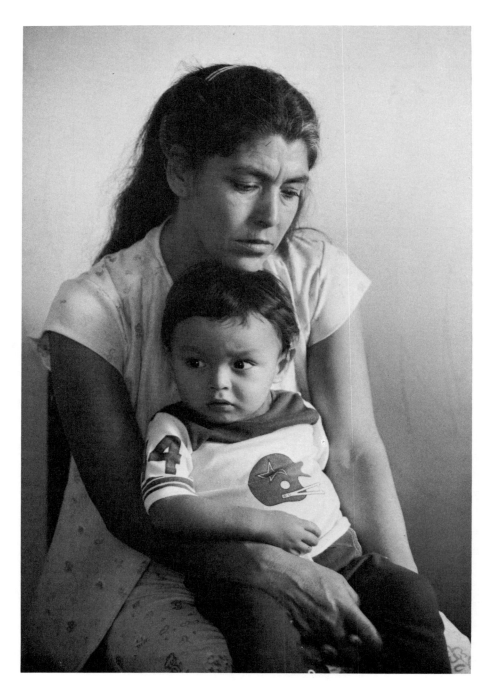

Migrant mother and child in Indiantown, Florida.

A SYSTEM IS evil that forces children to spend their lives in manual labor, that pays little attention to health and safety standards, that holds human beings in peonage, that welcomes illegal aliens because of the low wages they will take, that brings foreign laborers into the country to take jobs away from its citizens.

The system of farm migrancy in America does all of those things and more. The system exists because migrant farmworkers have no political voice and no power to organize for their own protection. They are the most vulnerable and exploitable workers in America, and they are the most exploited. No other working group in America is now subjected to the kind of nineteenth-century working-class abuses that are a part of the everyday life of agricultural migrants.

The conditions of farm migrancy can be improved only by government and by the great corporations that now control agriculture in America. The government can pass and enforce laws that will prevent illegal aliens from taking jobs away from American workers and that will prevent abuse of the H-2 "guest worker" law. It can strengthen the laws against child labor in agriculture and more effectively enforce the ones that now exist. It can make the minimum-wage law apply to workers on all farms. It can provide a more effective system of unemployment insurance for migrants. It can increase Head Start and other educational opportunities for migrant children. The Department of Labor can set and enforce health and safety standards for farmworkers that it has for years refused to do.

Government does not provide basic justice to migrant farmworkers because there is no political will to provide it and because of active lobbying against such improvements by agribusiness. To make life better in these ways for migrants would raise the price of vegetables and fruits slightly or cut into corporate profits. Neither solution seems to be politically acceptable.

Most people do not realize that American agriculture is controlled more and more every day by big business, including some of the largest national and international corporations. Corporations whose names we never associate with agriculture are very much in the business of growing and processing food: Aetna Life & Casualty, ARCO, Bank America Corporation, International Telephone and Telegraph, J. C. Penney, RCA Corporation, Standard Oil of California. These are but a few illustrative names. During the 1960s alone more than seven thousand corporations went into the growing and processing of food. Corporate names such as Campbell's, Del Monte, Dole, Duffy Mott, General Mills, Hunt's, Kraft, Libby's, and Stokeley-Van Camp have been household words for years. Thousands of others we seldom hear of or notice.

The food giants now control the majority of vegetables and fruits grown in America, and the percentage of control increases

A migrant picks oranges near Haines City, Florida.

each year. They either grow their own food for processing or contract for it with private growers. These companies have the power to set fair wages and enforce reasonable working and living conditions for migrants if they chose to do so.

Although stubborn about wage increases, some companies and growers' associations have shown concern for improvements in migrant housing and health care and for increased educational opportunities for migrant children. The majority, however, continue to turn their backs on migrants and deny their responsibility by hiding behind the farm labor contractor (crew leader) system.

Unfortunately, old, totally false attitudes persist among many people who should know better. They are embodied at their very worst in a statement made to Truman Moore *(The Slaves We Rent)* by the president of a multimillion-dollar grower-packer-shipper company: "Migrants are the scum of the earth. Anything they get over forty cents an hour is gravy."

That statement is extreme, but ignorance of migrant farmworkers is common among the corporate leaders who control American agriculture. If our book has shown anything, it is that migrant farmworkers are hardworking people with an elemental strength and toughness that make them a part of the bone and fiber of this country. They should be respected and rewarded fairly for the contributions they make to our society.

"We are a part of America," Estela Rodriguez said to me during one of our talks about migrants.

Estela is right, and America should not forget it.

Further Reading about Migrant Farmworkers

For readers who want to learn more about migrant farmworkers in America we have several suggestions. John Steinbeck's *The Grapes of Wrath* presents a picture of migrant agricultural workers during the Depression and Dust Bowl era that is still unforgettable after nearly half a century. *Hard Traveling* by Tony Dunbar and Linda Kravitz is a well-researched report on such subjects as conditions of migrant labor, the law and migrant justice, and who is making money in agribusiness.

Cesar Chavez: Man of Courage by Florence M. White tells the story of a Mexican-American migrant who, against great odds, formed a successful farmworkers labor union, the United Farm Workers, in California during the 1960s. Our *The New Americans* goes into considerable detail about illegal aliens, whose large numbers create many problems for legal U.S. migrant farmworkers. The Department of Agriculture publishes a yearbook about the food growing and processing industry in America. The 1982 yearbook, *Food—from Farm to Table,* is particularly interesting.

Index